MARCO ⊕ POLO
TUS

GW00492567

with Local Tips
*The author's special recommendations are
highlighted in yellow throughout this guide*

There are five symbols to help you find your way around this guide:

★

Marco Polo's top recommendations – the best in each category

⧸⧹⟋

sites with a scenic view

◉

places where the local people meet

⋏

places where young people get together

(104/A1)
pages and coordinates for the Road Atlas of Tuscany
(U/A1) *coordinates for the City Map of Florence inside back cover*
(O) *area not covered by the City Map*

MARCO ✦ POLO

Travel guides and language guides in this series:

Algarve • Amsterdam • Australia/Sydney • Berlin • Brittany • California
Canada • Channel Islands • Costa Brava/Barcelona • Costa del Sol/Granada
Côte d'Azur • Crete • Cuba • Cyprus • Dominican Republic • Eastern Canada
Eastern USA • Florence • Florida • Gran Canaria • Greek Islands/Aegean
Ibiza • Ireland • Istanbul • Lanzarote • London • Mallorca • Malta • Mexico
New York • New Zealand • Normandy • Paris • Prague • Rhodes • Rome
Scotland • South Africa • Southwestern USA • Tenerife • Turkish Coast
Tuscany • Venice • Western Canada

French • German • Italian • Spanish

*Marco Polo would be very interested to hear your
comments and suggestions. Please write to:*

North America:
Marco Polo North America
70 Bloor Street East
Oshawa, Ontario, Canada
(B) 905-436-2525

United Kingdom:
GeoCenter International Ltd
The Viables Centre
Harrow Way
Basingstoke, Hants RG22 4BJ

*Our authors have done their research very carefully, but should any errors or omissions
have occurred, the publisher cannot be held responsible for any injury, damage
or inconvenience suffered due to incorrect information in this guide*

Cover photograph: Contignano (Hamann: Straiton)
Photos: K. Kallabis (16); Lelli (18); Mauritius: Dumrath (68),
Friedmann (24), Gebhardt (59), Gierth (6), Hubatka (21, 43, 46, 80, 83, 90, 103),
Leinauer (35), Ligges (4, 11, 12, 14), Nebe (22), Photo Bank (9), Schwarz (56),
Thiele (62), Vidler (32); M. Schulte-Kellinghaus (51, 70); Transglobe: Hartmann (64)

2nd revised edition 2000
© Mairs Geographischer Verlag, Ostfildern, Germany
Author: Ursula Romig-Kirsch
Translator: Michael Grunwald
English edition 2000: Gaia Text
Editorial director: Ferdinand Ranft
Chief editor: Marion Zorn
Cartography for the Road Atlas: © Mairs Geographischer Verlag, Ostfildern
Istituto Geografico De Agostini, Novara
Design and layout: Thienhaus/Wippermann
Printed in Germany

CONTENTS

Discover Tuscany!

*Breathtaking countryside and a fascinating culture
ensure an unforgettable experience*

Much has been written about Tuscany – no other region of Italy is as familiar to us – and yet nowhere do we encounter so many surprises. It is no 'land of lemon blossoms', no lush, verdant countryside populated by lyrical peasants, but instead a somewhat harsh region, shaped and cultivated throughout the millennia by a proud and laconic people. Tuscany is one of the most densely wooded areas of Italy. In the Apennines one finds mixed forests of beech, oak, sweet chestnut and fir trees. The hinterland running along the 300-km coastline is shrouded with pine forests while the Mediterranean Macchia strip is blanketed by an impenetrable scrubland of holm oak, myrtle, gorse, erica, strawberry tree, and blackberry, the scent of the latter wafting enticingly across the countryside in the early summer months. Cork oaks abound to the south of the Cecina River. The high and low forests and the

Macchia cover an area totalling 870,000 hectares. The entire region is littered with reminders of previous volcanic activity, and mild earth tremors are no rarity in this day and age. But unlike in other parts of Italy, they have never caused significant damage here. Major geothermal activity has created thermal baths in an area extending from around Lucca to the southern Maremma. Only one-tenth of Tuscany consists of flat land and the mountainous peaks of the Apuan Alps and the Apennines reach altitudes of 2,000 m.

In the 6th and 7th centuries B.C. the Greeks introduced wine and olive growing to Italy. These ancient cultivated plants dominate the countryside south of Florence and surrounding Lucca. When this area was surveyed during Etruscan and Roman times cypress trees were used to separate and subdivide the land. Today they still give the region its distinctive appearance. As early as the Middle Ages Tuscany developed its distinctive character, reflecting the balance between man and nature, an intricate web of

*An old Tuscan farmhouse
in the hills: the long-awaited
dream of a simple life*

View over the rooftops of Florence to the Duomo and the Palazzo Vecchio

farmsteads and fortified towns and cities, cast over the landscape like a loose net.

The municipalities have been in direct competition since the early Middle Ages, a fact which partly explains the rather reserved character and somehow rough yet enchanting exterior of many of the people. Even today, most Tuscans feel an exclusive allegiance to their birthplace. A person born in Fiesole would never call himself a Florentine, although the largely unknown village is virtually a suburb of the city of Florence. Fuelled by the mutual dislike of their respective inhabitants, the cities of Florence and Prato are worlds apart, as are the small provincial towns, which were traditionally ruled by rival families. Just as strong is the allegiance felt toward one's own suburb. A prime example of such rivalry is the Palio delle Contrade, a fiercely contested horse race held annually in Siena between the city's 17 suburbs.

Very few Tuscans decide to emigrate; at most they move within the region. This may partially explain their intolerance towards immigrants from the south of Italy. Historically, Tuscany has always been known as a relatively densely populated region. Today one finds the highest concentration of people n the lower reaches of the Arno Valley and around Pisa and Livorno, with approximately 250–300 inhabitants per square kilometre. The provinces of Arezzo, Siena and especially Grosseto on the coast are less populated, with fewer than 50 inhabitants per square kilometre. Most strangers are greeted cordially by the local Tuscans, albeit in a somewhat restrained manner. Joviality or servility is unlikely to be encountered here. Those tourists accustomed to fawning service are likely to feel slightly neglected in Tuscany. This is, however, not the case; it is simply not a local custom to impose or intrude into another's private sphere. Spontaneous invitations to visit Tuscans within their own four walls will be a long time coming, apart from being offered a cup of coffee, so the age-old dilemma of what to wear on such occasions is almost entirely hypothetical. Should the occasion arise, however, one should tend toward simplicity and understatement. And while on the subject of clothing, do not forget to pack a warm sweater or cardigan, even in the middle of summer! Comfortable shoes are just as important as sandals, and the more adventurous may even care to carry rubber boots in their car.

Tuscany generally enjoys a mild Mediterranean climate and the winter months are largely sunny, but there are no shortage of very cold days and, with the *Tramontana* blowing in from the mountains, the temperature can drop to -12°C (10°F). Apart from the higher mountain reaches, snow is rare. Spring and autumn tend to be very mild (and are therefore recommended for travel) but tend to be precipitous. At times the coast experiences a very strong south-west wind, the *Libeccio*, and in August there are often severe thunderstorms. Particularly in July, the hottest month, temperatures can soar to 35°C (95°F) and above. At this time it tends to be oppressively humid in the more low-lying areas such as Florence and the Arno Valley. At least along the coast and at higher altitudes the evenings provide cool relief.

What fascinates most about Tuscany is the amazing variety of the landscape. In the words of the traveller Théophile Gautier in 1850: 'An azure blue panorama of plains, mountains, and valleys; scattered towns and country houses along the horizon in an interplay of light and shadow' – and this is still the visitor's initial impression today. One then learns that the best time to visit the southern coastal lowlands of the Maremma is at the height of summer and that the Chianti offers its finest when the vine leaves assume a bright red hue. The forest near Camaldoli reaches the height of its suggestive powers when it is swathed in an early morning fog and the *balze* near Volterra are best viewed at sunset, when the shades of the multicoloured layers of earth are most visible. Unfortunately, one does not always have an opportunity to visit each spot during its optimal season, but planning should definitely be done with such aspects in mind. Late autumn and winter are the best times for visiting

History at a glance

About 1000 B.C.
Etruscans invade present day Tuscany

About 300 B.C.
The Etruscans relinquish their supremacy to Rome

89 B.C.
Roman citizenship granted to all Italic peoples

568 A.D.
The Lombards elevate Tuscien to the status of margravate and reside in Lucca

774
Frank rule begins

About 1000
Margrave Hugo moves the Tuscan seat of government to Florence

1139–1266
Tuscany under Hohenstaufen imperial rule; creation of the city states

13th–14th centuries
Conflict between the Ghibelline and Guelph, supporters of the imperial and papal parties respectively; the Florentines extend their power to include the cities of Prato, Pistoia, Arezzo, San Gimignano, Volterra and Cortona

1252
First gold florin (Florin d'oro) minted in Florence

1406
Florence subjugates Pisa

15th–16th centuries
Renaissance: Culture flourishes in the region under the Medici in Florence

1555
Florence conquers Siena

1737
Gian Gastone, the last Medici Grand Duke, dies and Tuscany falls to the Austrian House of Lorraine

1799
Napoleon conquers Tuscany

1815–59
The Lorraine return to Tuscany

1860
Tuscany joins the Kingdom of Italy following a referendum

1865–71
Florence is the capital of Italy

1946
Following its defeat in World War II, Italy decides in a referendum to become a republic

1970
Tuscany established as a region, with Florence as the capital and encompassing the provinces Arezzo, Florence, Grosseto, Livorno, Lucca, Massa-Carrara, Pisa, Pistoia, Siena and, since 1992, Prato

museums and whiling away the hours shopping, as views of the sights are not blocked by endless groups of tourists and service staff tend to be especially polite. In January and February the silver wattles and almond trees are in full blossom along the coast and one can enjoy uninterrupted walks along a beach broached by a churning sea, which has a special appeal. At Easter time the area to visit is southern Tuscany, which offers exceptional contrasts. Red clover carpets the hilly slopes, while snow still lies on the peak of Mount Amiata. May is probably the best time for walking tours through the deep valleys of the Garfagnana region or at higher altitudes in the Apuan Alps or through the volcanic landscape surrounding Mount Amiata, rich with abundant and diverse flora and fauna.

There is an extensive range of wildlife in Tuscany: deer, roe-deer, and especially in the Maremma region, wild boar. Almost everywhere there are badgers, foxes, martens and polecats. In some areas there are porcupines and land tortoises, and occasionally at high altitude in the Apennines a confused wolf may even cross your path. In May the nightingales break into song and in June the olive groves are inundated by millions of fireflies.

The waters of the Tuscan archipelago are very popular with yachtsmen. Numerous renowned sailing regattas are held annually in summer along this coast, which is dotted with luxuriously equipped harbours.

The islands with their many cliffs and bays are a paradise for underwater fishermen and divers. Bathing along the beautiful sandy beaches, stretching over many kilometres of the Versilia, is a particularly fashionable pastime. Not only do the most elegant women of Floren-

Porto Azzurro harbour on Elba

tine high society populate these beaches, but exquisite nightclubs, wild discos, and expensive restaurants stand wall to wall along the boardwalk. South of Pisa beach life becomes more relaxed and family-oriented, while along the rocky coastline near Mount Argentario the rich and famous enjoy their isolation. Elba is the most popular destination for German tourists and Giglio tends to attract Italians. During August the entire coastline becomes inundated by Tuscans as well as Romans and the beaches are rather full. By September and October the coastline is once again left in the care of foreign tourists and it is never better than in these golden days of late summer! Grape-picking is just starting in the wine regions and for those wishing to spend some peaceful days in one of the refurbished estates or in one of the charming Chianti castles, now is the perfect time. From November to January the *brucatura* takes place, when the olives are brushed from the branches by hand, although sometimes this work is being done mechanically.

In Tuscany 195,000 hectares of land are dedicated to growing olives. Although the region is ranked fourth in Italy with respect to oil production, many connoisseurs consider it to be superior to its rivals. In addition to the fine wines (DOC and DOCG) originating chiefly from the Chianti area, high quality olive oil is one of the region's major agricultural exports.

Industrial manufacturing plays a minor role in Tuscany, notwithstanding the iron smelting in Piombino, the shipyards and refineries in Livorno, and the various chemical plants in the region. Even in the wake of the economic renaissance in the 1960s the region's businesses retained their distinctive form: small, dynamic firms and workshops enjoying maximum independence. They are situated in centres well located for accessing raw materials, their position attributable to their traditional roots. Outstanding examples of this are the textile production and silk weaving in Prato and Lucca.

How is life in Tuscany? According to statistics, fairly good. The per capita income is well above the national average and there are no slums in the industrial suburbs. However, the harmony between man and nature which was achieved over thousands of years is slowly fading to nothing more than a myth. The historical city centres, originally designed for considerably lower densities, are becoming increasingly inhospitable for human habitation, despite efforts to divert traffic away from them. Tourism, with its diverse and heavy demands, is also contributing to this demise. Paradoxically, it is this tourism that stimulates the desperate attempts to halt such decay.

The beauty of the region and, above all, the art treasures to be found in its cities attract well over seven million visitors annually, with Tuscany being one of the most popular tourist destinations in all of Europe. It encompasses the greatest art collection in Italy, with 80 per cent of the country's art treasures found within its borders. Few regions have inseminated European art and culture to the extent Tuscany has. However, Tuscany doesn't feel like a museum; names such as Botticelli, Donatello, Leonardo, Michelangelo, Dante, Boccaccio, Petrarca, Machiavelli and Galilei are as familiar to Tuscans as the names of their own friends, so they are simply treated as 'departed neighbours'.

But modernization is slowly creeping into Tuscany. At the end of 1998, all ten provinces formed an initiative under the motto 'Arte in Toscana – verso il Contemporaneo'. The aim is to give contemporary art a larger forum. In the past Tuscans have tended to rest solely on the laurels of historic art. A modest start had been made in Florence with the Museo Marino Marini, the

Fondazione Primo Conti in Fiesole, and the extensions to the Stazione Leopolda for exhibitions of modern art. A Centro d'Arte Contemporaneo in the old Rifredi textile factory is on the drawing board, too. But the only really important museums of modern art in the region are to be found solely in Prato (Centro per l'Arte Contemporanea Luigi Pecci) and in Santomato near Pistoia, where the open-air museum Fattoria di Celle was created but which has previously only been accessible to specialists. And Siena is currently installing a museum for contemporary art with video library, cyber café and internet access for visitors in the Palazzo delle Papesse.

The irrepressible Tuscan pride is founded on the artistic and cultural legacy of the region, unique not only due to its incomparable beauty, but also to this beauty being rooted in the collective consciousness of its inhabitants, to such an extent that they consider themselves its custodian. These people hate immoderation and gluttony in any form. One does not gorge oneself on the Romantic, Gothic, cities or monasteries, but makes a careful and measured selection, examining the chosen object in detail. Both the landscape and people demand reverence, and it is precisely this challenge that makes a holiday in Tuscany such an unforgettable experience.

A farmstead encircled by cypresses: the epitome of rural Tuscany

11

From Chianti to marble

*Whether culinary or cultural:
generous servings for all*

Alabaster

Alabaster and Volterra are synonymous. Formed into 'pearls' weighing hundreds of kilos over thousands of years, this white to brownish-grey, crystallized calcium sulphate is quarried in the vicinity of the ancient Etruscan city of Volterra and fashioned in over 100 workshops, many of which have been owned and run by the same families for generations.

Apennines

Extending along the entire length of the Italian peninsula, from the Po Valley in the north to the craggy, forested mountains of Aspromonte in Calabria in the south, this lofty cordillera cannot be circumvented. The Tuscan Apennines are crossed by three major roads: the A15 Autostrada from Parma to La Spezia in the far north (over the Cisa Pass), the A1 Autostrada from Bologna to Florence (Futa Pass near Bologna), and the old Brenner Highway (S12) from Modena to Lucca. To reach the Adriatic coast from Florence you take the S67 to Forli over the Muraglione Pass. To get there from southern Tuscany you cross the Cerventosa Pass near Cortona, which is on your way to Perugia. All the passes are approximately 1,000 m above sea level.

Apuan Alps

The Apuan Alps rise almost directly from the sea between La Spezia and Viareggio to altitudes of 1,945 m above sea level (Monte Pisano). In spring they offer a breathtaking, snow-capped backdrop to the blue of the Ligurian Sea and the dense chesnut forests which extend halfway up the range. In summer the brilliant white cliffs of the marble quarries are often mistaken by tourists for snowfields. At the base of the Apuanian Alps, which are technically foothills of the Apennines, one finds the elegant seaside resorts of the Versilia.

Tuscan Archipelago

The term Tuscan Archipelago refers to the islands located off the mainland in the Tyrrhenian Sea.

Sheep grazing under an olive tree

In 1996 these rugged islands with their small sandy beaches and sheer cliffs were declared a national park, the Parco Nazionale dell'Arcipelago Toscano, which today encompasses a total area of around 75,000 hectares, including the surrounding marine areas.

Good tourist facilities are to be found on Elba (224 km²), Giglio (21.2 km²) and Capraia (20 km²). Pianosa, 'the flat one', is still a prison colony and not usually open to visitors. The northernmost island, Gorgona (2.2 km²), was also used for similar purposes until quite recently.

And then there is the craggy island of Montecristo, made world famous by Alexander Dumas's novel *The Count of Monte Christo*, and the tiny island of Giannutri, which features the remnants of a Roman villa (today private property).

What grows together, belongs together: Sangiovese + Canaiolo = Chianti

Chianti

The much-lauded home of the Chianti Classico is a hilly region in the geographic centre of Tuscany. It covers 80,000 hectares and is subdivided into over 700 vineyards. Forty-five per cent of its total area, which extends from Florence to Siena, is covered by forest. As early as 1444 the towns of Radda, Gaiole and Castellina formed the Lega del Chianti, which lay down strict rules governing the quality of wine produced here. Then in 1874 Baron Bettino Ricasoli prescribed the ratios to be observed when combining grape varieties to produce Gallo Nero (black cockerel), the region's premium blend. These specifications remain almost unchanged today, with wines bearing the black cockerel seal of quality on their necks consisting of 75–90 per cent Sangiovese grapes, 5–15 per cent Canaiolo (for the typical ruby red hue) and a maximum of 10 per cent from the white varieties Malvasia or Trebbiano.

In recent years, however, some of the more experimental vintners have challenged these rigid regulations, leading to an apparent contradiction: a Chianti made solely from the expensive Sangiovese grapes, which has been given the DOC (*Denominazione di Origine Controllata*) seal, is marketed as a modest-sounding table wine (*vino da tavola*). So don't be surprised if you're charged considerably more for a 'table wine' of this ilk than for a DOC Chianti sporting the famous cockerel.

Following the war the Chianti experienced a sad decline as a result of rural emigration and general negligence. But with the commitment of the long established producers and an influx of young entrepreneurs equipped with modern technology, it has now regained its former position as the king of Italy's wines. This renaissance has also seen the refurbishment of many of the dilapidated farm houses, which have been established as hotels or holiday apartments, largely by northern and central Europeans.

Etruscans

Prior to their final defeat at the hands of the Romans in 265 B.C., these enigmatic people whose origins have still not been fully explained populated extensive areas of central Italy, which they named Etruria, from around 1000 B.C. until their demise. One region situated primarily in modern Tuscany was known as Tuscien and extended along the coast. Of the cities within Tuscany, Arezzo, Chiusi, Populonia, Roselle, Vetulonia and Volterra were members of the Dodecapolis, a confederation of the 12 most powerful city states formed in 600 B.C. But numerous other towns, such as Ansedonia, Cortona and Fiesole, also testify to past influences exerted on them by Etruscan culture. Extensive collections are to be found in the Museo Archeologico in Florence, the Museo Guarnacci in Volterra and the Etruscan National Museum in Chiusi. Significant necropoli (grave sites) are located in Populonia and Sovana.

Giglio

Italian for 'lily', it not only denominates the most beautiful island of the Tuscan archipelago, but also the heraldic flower of Florence (a red lily on a white background) and the ubiquitous bluish-purple iris which grows in abundance along the walls in spring.

Marble

Above Carrara, which lends its name to the famous white marble, lie the marble quarries of Colonnata, Fantiscritti und Ravaccione. It is primarily the fine-grained *bianco di Carrara* which has captivated sculptors since Michelangelo and which is hewn in the form of massive blocks directly from the cliffs here. These *bancata* can be up to 12 m in height and may weigh up to 400 tonnes! Moore, Botero, Pomo-

From a distance Carrara's marble quarries look like they are covered with snow

doro, Marini and numerous others have commissioned workshops in Pietrasanta to shape them into the sculptures which now decorate museums around the world. The marble quarries may be visited without special permission – but for obvious reasons, a certain degree of care should be exercised!

Medici

This family of merchants, bankers, and princes first ruled over Florence from the end of the 14th century and then over all of Tuscany until 1737. The most prominent members of the Medici clan were Cosimo il Vecchio (1389–1464), who laid the foundation for their incredible wealth and their art collections, his grandson Lorenzo the Magnificent (1449–1492), who was largely responsible for broadening their trade relationships, and Grand Duke Cosimo I (1519–1574), whose many achievements included commissioning the Uffizi in Florence and giving the state its modern form. And, of course, one cannot forget Anna Maria

Ludovica, the last of the Medici, who left the family's entire collection of art treasures 'in perpetuity' to the people of Florence in 1737. It is to her that the city of Florence owes its gratitude for today's huge museum collections.

Renaissance

Rinascimento, or 'rebirth' in Italian, is a ubiquitous term in Tuscany. In the middle of the 15th century a cultural movement developed here which sought to reinstate classical ideals in philosophy and art. All things noble, truthful and beautiful were idealized, with humans epitomizing these qualities. Florence established itself as the focal point of this movement. While the notion of a spiritual afterlife had been dominant during the Gothic period, the Renaissance ushered in a period in which mortal man became the measure for all endeavours in art and philosophy.

Vineyards

Tuscany is one of the leading grape growing regions of Italy. Of the 150 vineyards which formed the Movimento per il Turismo del Vino in early 1994, 118 are to be found in Tuscany. The vineyards listed below can be visited, but it is advisable to telephone beforehand. On the island of Elba the *Azienda Acquabona* is known for its excellent Aleatico, the local sweet wine *(Portoferraio; Tel. 05 65 93 30 13)*. In southern Tuscany the *Cantine Contucci* has established its cellars within the old city walls of *Montepulciano (Via Teatro, 1; Tel. 05 78 75 70 06)*, and the *Cantina del Redi (Via Collazzi, 5; Tel. 05 78 75 71 66)*. Both vineyards grow the famous Vino Nobile di Montepulciano. In nearby *Montalcino* the annual *Fattoria dei Barbi* literature award is presented for works concerning wine. This *fattoria's* wine is among the best in the area *(Suburb of Podernovi; Tel. 05 77 84 82 77)*. The Vino Rosso di Montalcino is also produced, among other places, at the *Fattoria dell'Altesino* vineyard, an imposing fortress *(Suburb of Altesino; Tel. 05 77 80 62 08)*, and at *Villa Banfi (Castello di Poggio alle Mura; Tel. 05 77 84 01 11)*. In the Villa Banfi, with its somewhat futuristic cellars, there is also a small public glass museum. For those interested, a visit to the *Azienda della Pieve di S. Restituta* in the picturesque suburb of the same name can be recommended *(Tel. 05 77 84 86 10)*.

Between Florence and Siena lies the Chianti Classico region. The *Castello di Volpaia*, its cellars filled with massive oak and chestnut barrels, is situated in a medieval hamlet *(Radda in Chianti; Tel. 05 77 73 80 66)*. The castle and vineyards of *Castello di Fonterutoli* are among the oldest in the region and have been owned and run by the same family since 1435 *(Castellina in Chianti; Tel. 05 77 74 04 76)*. A *vitarium* containing all grape varieties found in Tuscany has been established in the vineyard of *S. Felice*, in the vicinity of the medieval village of S. Gusmè *(Tel. 05 77 35 90 87)*. The *Castello di Monsanto* is connected to the grape-crushing and pressing plant by a tunnel and is used as a wine cellar *(Barberino Val d'Elsa; Tel. 05 58 05 90 00)*. Even Leonardo da Vinci spent time at *Castello di Vignamaggio* and most surely indulged in the odd drop of the noble *vino rosso* on occasion *(Greve in Chianti; Tel. 055 85 35 59)*.

Not members of the Movimento per il Turismo del Vino, but still well worth a visit are the *Fattoria di Rampolla,* owned by Prince Di Napoli Rampolla *(Panzano in Chianti; Tel. 055 85 20 01)*, and of course the *Castello di Brolio*, owned since 1141 by the Barons of Ricasole, leading advocates for the recognition of Chianti wine *(Gaiole in Chianti; Tel. 05 77 73 01)*.

You can savour an excellent Vernaccia di S. Gimignano, the Terre di Tufo, at the *Fattoria Ponte a Rondolino Teruzzi e Puthod* with a fully computerized cellar *(Località Casale; Tel. 05 77 94 01 43)*.

Of particular note is an all female initiative founded in 1988 by vineyard proprietors at *Villa Vistarenni*, the property of Elisabetta Tognana and one of the most enchanting castles in the Chianti region *(Gaiole in Chianti; Also 3 attractive holiday apartments; Tel. 05 77 73 84 76)*. Their group, the Associazione Nazionale Donne del Vino, now has over 250 members.

From antipasti to wild boar

Tuscan cuisine reflects each particular environment and season

Food

Eating is an Italian passion involving many hours of indulgence, preferably in the company of a large circle of friends. Each individual region has its own particular specialties, with everything from fish to game, from mushrooms to green asparagus, and from artichokes to chestnuts prepared fresh in the traditional manner. Tuscany is renowned for its superb olive oil and tasty *pecorino* (sheep's milk cheese) from its rural pastures in the south. Along the coast you can enjoy a range of seafood dishes. Feel free to ask the chefs to show you your fish before preparation – they're usually more than happy to do so. Fish tends to be a little on the expensive side, but other seafood (apart from lobster) may be less pricey, such as *zuppa di cozze* (mussel soup), *frittura mista* (mixed, deep-fried seafood) and *cacciucco*, Livorno's famous fish soup.

Especially in and around Florence *bistecca alla fiorentina* is a long-standing favourite: a huge, thick T-bone steak from local Chianina cattle, seasoned and grilled over a wood fire. The price for *bistecca* is almost always quoted on the menu in terms of *per etto*, i.e. per 100 g – and a true *bistecca* tips the scales at around 800 g and is a couple of inches thick! In the area around Arezzo a traditional favourite is *scottiglia*, a type of goulash; the pride of Pistoia's culinary heritage are various *frattaglie* dishes (offal). From Siena to Maremma the locals love meat and sausages seasoned with locally grown tarragon as well as wild boar *(cinghiale)* with raisins and pine nuts. There are also the tasty *fagioli all'uccelletto*, white beans with spicy, coarse fried sausages. In Colonnata in the Apuan Alps the locals leave sides of bacon maturing in sea salt and various herbs in marble vats for months, before slicing them thinly and serving them as a delicious entrée. *Crostini*, roasted slices of bread smothered with liver paste, make a superb starter. But one should not overlook *fettunta*, toasted slices of white bread rubbed with garlic and sprinkled with freshly pressed, aromatic olive oil. Together with a glass of new wine –

Vineyard picnic: an afternoon in the lap of rusticity

unforgettable! The selection of *verdura, insalate e contorni* (vegetables, salads and side dishes – never pasta) depends largely on available local supplies and is seasonally determined. Vegetables are often braised and refined with a little unheated olive oil.

Although pasta dishes are not traditionally Tuscan (they originated in southern Italy) you definitely shouldn't pass up the opportunity of enjoying *primo piatti* (first courses) *tagliatelle al cinghiale* (flat, broad noodles with wild boar ragout) or *spaghetti alle vongole* (spaghetti with mussels) if they appear on the menu. Particularly appetizing are the *zuppe* or *minestre*, a wide range of soups, but particularly *minestrone*, which is a vegetable soup containing pasta or rice.

And then, of course, all those desserts! In the north during the colder months chestnut flour is used for making *castagnaccio*, a cake with rosemary and pine nuts, and for *lecci di Garfagnana* (pancakes filled with soft curd cheese). Prato produces the renowned *biscotti di Prato*, a double-baked almond biscuit, and *panforte* (marzipan bread with candied fruits and nuts), while from Siena come *ricciarelli* (marzipan biscuits).

The customary sequence of courses is generally: *antipasto* (entrée – mostly cold), *primo piatto* (first course of soup, rice or pasta), *secondo piatto* (main course – meat or fish with side dish of vegetables or salad), *formaggio* (cheese) or/and *dolce* (dessert), *caffè*, and maybe a *digestivo*. Of course, you can shorten this sequence, but in restaurants it is nearly impossible to order only a pasta dish and nothing else; however, it is more acceptable to do so in the more basic *trattorie*. If you're after fast food there are *tavole calde* (self-serve restaurants), *pizzerie* or *spaghetterie*. In restaurants and *trattorie* you have to pay between L3,000 and L10,000 per person for *pane e coperto* (literally 'bread and cover'), the exact price for this appearing on the menu. It is advisable to actually see the menu before ordering, as in both simple as well as expensive establishments it is not uncommon for the waiter to rattle off the courses at lightning speed in local dialect. This can sometimes result in unpleasant surprises. The bill is always issued for the whole table, so if you plan on going Dutch, it's best to have one person pay and reimburse them later. And remember that restaurants can charge up to 16 per cent for service *(servizio)* on top of the cost of the meal before you complain about the waiter's maths.

Dining in a restaurant in Italy is not cheap, but a meal in a typical *trattoria* really is a must. In larger cities you also find fixed menus for tourists *(menù turistici)*; with everything included they cost around L25,000–35,000, and consist of three courses. Overall, while they generally provide value for money, they don't have much in common with classic Tuscan cuisine. Cheaper – and often better – is a pizza with a glass of the local *vino da tavola*. As far as breakfast is concerned, it can safely be said that it deviates somewhat from its traditional British or North American counterpart. But when in Rome (or Tuscany) – you can definitely get used to it! Just find the closest bar and order a *cappuccino* and a *brioche* (soft bread croissant). You

A wine merchant near Pitigliano, where the bianco vines grow on tuff

either order and pay at the bar, or first order and pay a cashier near the door, who then provides you with a receipt to present at the bar, where you order again. Basically, the only breakfasts which fulfil one's non-Mediterranean expectations are those served in 5-star hotels or in hotels with half-board. By the way, an Italian bar is more like a café which also serves alcoholic beverages, which is not to be confused with a piano bar, a more nocturnal establishment.

Drinks

Acqua (water), *acqua minerale gassata* (carbonated mineral water) or *acqua non gassata* (non-carbonated mineral water) is drunk with every meal. Of the red wines, it is of course the Chianti which tops the list in popularity, and especially the Chianti Classico produced in the region between Florence and Siena. The red Chianti wines from the hills around Siena and to the north of Arezzo are also full-bodied, as are the Chianti

Putto from the Sieve Valley and the reds from Carmignano and Montalbano in the lower Arno Valley. The most famous red wines include the Brunello from Montalcino, Vino Nobile di Montepulciano and – above all – Sassicaia and Ornellaia from Bolgheri. Famous white wines include the golden Vernaccia from San Gimignano, the recently-created and light Galestro, the Bianco di Montecarlo, and Bianco Vergine, the 'virgin' white from the area around Cortona. Dessert wines of note are Vino Santo, Moscato and the strong, sweet wines from Elba. Italians tend to drink wine only with meals; it is often a house wine *(vino di casa* or *vino aperto)* rather than a more expensive bottled wine. After a meal one may perhaps imbibe a *digestivo* or whisky – but just one. Italians drink in moderation as insobriety is a sign of a lack of masculinity or weakness. Young children tend to drink water or soft drinks with their meals.

21

Ceramics, leather and olive oil

Italian fashion and food markets to tempt the eye

For centuries Florence, Lucca, and Prato have enjoyed a global reputation for their exquisite materials, and leather goods are a specialty of the lower Arno Valley, home to long-established tanneries. Fashionable footwear and accessories tend to be *numero uno* on vacation shopping lists for Tuscany. Florence is headquarters to many large fashion houses such as Ferragamo, Gucci, Pucci, Coveri etc. But be selective, as the clothing prices vary incredibly, with some articles clearly overpriced. All the same, whether expensive or not, Italian fashion is unique in its enigmatic blend of refined yet simple elegance.

Rummaging at markets is a beloved pastime. Every village and every city has its weekly market offering clothing, linen, household items, fruit, vegetables, plants and groceries. Olive oil and wine should, however, be purchased from the producer at a *fattoria* or *enoteca* – they are also able to dispatch goods to your home address directly and in large quantities. For the avid shopper on the lookout for agricultural produce your best bet is probably Siena and environs, as well as the Maremma region. Monks purvey self-distilled herb-flavoured liqueur and honey directly from their monasteries. Siena, Cortona and the region around Montelupo, west of Florence, are also well-known for their brightly-coloured glazed ceramics.

Florence is famous for its silverware, while Arezzo has a reputation for gold craftsmanship. Volterra is the place for alabaster, while Carrara and environs is a good area to look for marble objects. Pistoia is known for knives and steel products, as well as for supplying tree nurseries throughout the world. There are notable antique markets in Arezzo, Lucca and Pisa. Shops are usually open Monday–Friday from 8.30 am–12.30 pm and 4 pm–7.30 pm, but in city centres they tend to stay open throughout the whole day, often with no set opening and closing times.

Tuscany's many markets offer everything from the practical to the curious

23

Horse racing and jazz concerts

The highlight of the season is the bareback horse race around Siena's famous Campo

Life in Tuscany is accompanied by an annual cycle of musical and theatrical festivals, historical costume pageants, and above all, by *sagre*, the innumerable local village festivals, both small and large. Troupes of wandering minstrels and entertainers appear everywhere throughout the summer months, providing traditional, yet thrilling theatre performances. Religious celebrations in Tuscany tend to be conducted with customary reserve. Information regarding exact dates of festivals and performances can be obtained from the APT (Tourist Promotion Authority) in the provincial capitals.

PUBLIC HOLIDAYS

1 January *(Capodanno)*; 6 January *(Epifania)*; Easter *(Pasqua)*; Easter Monday *(Pasquetta)*; 25 April *(Liberazione)*; 1 May *(Festa del Lavoro)*; 15 August *(Ferragosto)*; 1 November *(Ognissanti)*; 8 December *(Immacolata Concezione)*; 25 December *(Natale)*; Boxing Day *(S. Stefano)*. The name-day of each village's patron

The Palio in Siena is won by the steed and not the jockey

saint is a *semifestivo*, i.e. shops remain closed in the afternoon.

FESTIVALS & LOCAL EVENTS

February
Carnevale di Viareggio
Carnival procession on Shrove Tuesday with amusing floats inspired by local themes

Easter Sunday
Scoppio del Carro
The 'Explosion of the Carriage' is a religious and folkloric ceremony held on the Piazza del Duomo in Florence on Easter Sunday.
Presentazione del Sacro Cingolo
Prato's festival procession and display of the 'Sacred Cloak' (also 1 May, 15 Aug, 8 Sept, 25 Dec)

April–June
Maggio Musicale Fiorentino
Florence's international music festival with dance and fringe events
Sagra Musicale Lucchese
Festival of sacred music held in Lucca's numerous churches

Mid June–Late August
Estate Fiesolana
A music, theatre, dance and film festival for two-and-a-half months

MARCO POLO SELECTION: FESTIVALS

1 Palio in Siena
This horse race inside the Campo is the most thrilling and most colourful pageant in all of Italy (page 26)

2 Regata di S. Ranieri in Pisa
Traditional Arno regatta in full costume (page 26)

3 Giostra del Saracino
Arrezo's beautiful piazza provides the backdrop for this historical jousting tournament (page 27)

4 Calcio in Costume
Football as it was played in Florence in the 16th century (page 26)

in the green hill town of Fiesole north of Florence

17 June
★ *Regata di S. Ranieri*
Colourful regatta on the Arno in Pisa. After dark its riverside buildings are illuminated.

24 June (San Giovanni)
★ *Calcio in Costume*
Historical game of Renaissance football usually held on the Piazza di Santa Croce in Florence

Final Sunday of June
✪♣ *Gioco del Ponte*
A relict of the late Middle Ages, the 'Game of the Bridge' began in 1568.

Early July
♣ *Bluesin*
A major Blues festival held in Pistoia over three days

2 July and 16 August
Palio delle Contrade in Siena
★ Ten horses and riders complete three gruelling circuits of the Piazza del Campo. In 1998 two horses actually died, giving animal protectionists reason to protest yet again, but every year

the Palio attracts over 70,000 keen spectators.

Every year since the Middle Ages ten of the 17 *contrade* (municipal districts) win the right to enter a rider (mostly from the Maremma or Sardinia) in the Palio. On each of the three days prior to the race, trial runs are conducted at 7. pm and 7.30 pm. On the eve of the Palio there is a final rehearsal and *la cena della prova generale,* the main pageant feast attended by all *contrade.* On the morning of race day there is the *provaccia,* a final run. Preparations begin on the Piazza del Campo at 5.20 pm and the actual race starts at 7.30 pm, lasting only about 90 seconds. The winning *contrada* receives the *palio,* a banner bearing an image of the Madonna, while the victorious horse (not the jockey!) is given pride of place at the ensuing celebratory feast.

Mid July
Festival Internazionale di Jazz Grey Cat Music
Jazz in Grosseto
  Luglio Pistoiese
Summer festival in Pistoia featuring the major Italian blues and rock

music festival *Pistoia Blues*
   Estate Sangimignanese
Concert and opera performances on the cathedral square in San Gimignano
   ☫ *Umbria Jazz*
Held in Perugia in Umbria, this jazz festival attracts international musicians. Its influence extends over the regional boundary to Cortona in eastern Tuscany.
   Volterrateatro
Theatre performances on Volterra's many squares

25 July
Giostra dell'Orso
Historical parade and jousting tournament in Pistoia

July–August
Festival Internazionale dell'Attore
Contemporary theatre in Montalcino
   Cantiere Internazionale
Theatre and music workshop initiated by the composer Hans Werner Henze in Montepulciano
   Festival Pucciniano
Opera, concert and ballet by Puccini at Lago di Massaciuccoli, situated between Viareggio and Pisa
   ❖ *Teatro Povero di Monticchiello*
An entire village creates a play and performs it
   ❖ *Siena Jazz*
Jazz courses and concerts

Second Sunday of August
Balestro del Girifalco
Crossbow archery in 13th-century costumes in Massa Marittima

15 August
❖ *Sagra della Bistecca in Cortona*
Beefsteak Festival and markets

Mid/Late August
❖☫ *Settimana Musicale Senese*
The renowned Accademia Musicale Chigiana performs opera, symphonies and chamber music at various venues in Siena.

Final Sunday of August
★ *Giostra del Saracino*
Eight jousters in full regalia charge at the effigy of a Saracen on the Piazza Grande in Arezzo (also on first Sunday of September).
   ❖ *Bravio delle Botti*
Local inhabitants of Montepulciano attempt to roll heavy barrels of wine up the hill, after which the barrels are drunk dry.

First Sunday of September
❖ *Fiera del Cacio*
Sheep's cheese festival in Pienza

13 September
❖ *Processione del Volto Santo*
Grand procession through the torchlit streets of Lucca

Final Sunday of September
❖ *Festa dell'Uva in Impruneta*
The largest wine festival in the Chianti region

From late September
Biennale di Firenze
Fashion and art exhibitions and events over several weeks every second year (even years)

14–21 October
❖ *Fiera di S. Luca in Impruneta*
The largest market in Tuscany

Last three weekends in November
❖ *Sagra del Tartufo in S. Miniato*
An abundance of those much sought-after white truffles

SHORT TOUR

☛ **City Map inside back cover**

(118/B3-4) The city (pop. 380,000), located on both sides of the Arno River, is unique for many reasons; no other city can lay claim to so many important artists nor to so many works of art, palaces, monasteries, churches, convents and museums. And only few cities can offer so many fine boutiques and so many enticing markets in such a concentrated area. The entire inner city is off limits to private vehicles, so it makes sense to travel to Florence by train or bus and then simply walk. There are, however, large subterranean parking lots at the main S. Maria Novella train station and near the Piazza della Libertà.

VIEW OVER THE CITY

You get a wonderful view from ↘ *Piazzale Michelangelo* **(U/F6)** and from ↘ *Forte di Belvedere* **(U/C6)**, both on the left-hand (south-west) side of the Arno, especially at dusk.

SIGHTS & MUSEUMS

Duomo (Cathedral of Santa Maria del Fiore), Baptistery and Campanile **(U/C-D3)**

Behind the celebrated doors of the octagonal, green and white marble *Battistero* (Baptistery), consecrated in 1059, there is a larger-than-life mosaic of Christ and an exquisite marble floor. The *Duomo* was erected between 1296 and 1368, but the Neo-Gothic façade was only completed in 1887. The massive dome, the silhouette of which dominates the city, was constructed from 1420-34. Climb the 414 steps of Giotto's Gothic ↘ *Campanile* to be rewarded with a unique view! *Open summer 9 am – 6.50 pm, Winter 9 am–4.20 pm daily*

Museo Archeologico **(U/E2)**

In addition to Etruscan and Egyptian relics, one can view prehistoric, Greek and Roman artefacts. The collection is one of the largest in Italy. *Open 9 am–2 pm Tue–Sat, 9 am–1 pm Sun; Via della Colonna, 36*

Museo Nazionale del Bargello **(U/D4)**

The largest collection of Italian sculptures from the 14th to 16th centuries is held in the high vaulted rooms of this 13th-century palace, including works by Donatello, Michelangelo, Cellini and Giambologna. The major arms and armour, small bronze and majolica (hand-painted ceramic) collections of the Medici are also on display. *Open 8.30 am–1.50 pm Sat, Sun, Mon and Wed, 8.30 am–4 pm Tue, Thu and Fri; Via del Proconsolo, 4*

Museo dell'Opera del Duomo **(U/D3)**

On show here are those originals removed from the Duomo, Baptistery and Campanile, as well as all the plans, tools and projects related to the construction of these edifices. *Open 9 am–6 pm Mon–Sat; Piazza del Duomo*

Museo di S. Marco **(U/D1)**

Fra Angelico, a Dominican monk, adorned the cells, refectory and corridors of this monastery with world-renowned frescos between 1435–45. In the library one finds codexes, miniatures and handwritten documents. *Open 8.30 am–1.50 pm Sat–Mon, 8.30 am– 4 pm Tue, Thu and Fri; Piazza S. Marco, 3*

Museo di Storia della Scienza (U/D5)

A wide range of scientific devices, instruments and curiosities from the Renaissance to the 20th century, and a significant mineral collection. *Open 9.30 am–1 pm Mon–Sat, also 2 pm–5 pm Mon, Wed and Fri; Piazza dei Giudici, 1*

Palazzo Pitti (U/B6)

You will need an entire day to visit all seven museums housed in this monumental palace. The 🜨 ☯ *Giardino di Boboli*, one of the most impressive gardens in Italy, extends up the slope behind the palace. *Galleria Palatina open 8.30 am–6.50 pm Tue–Sat, 8.30 am–1.50 pm Sun, also 8.30 pm–11.30 pm Fri, garden until sunset*

Piazza della Signoria (U/C–D4)

☯ ⚔ This busy Piazza is dominated by the Gothic *Palazzo Vecchio* with its 94 m tower. Florence has been governed from this palace since the 14th century. You can climb the 🜨 *tower* (great view!) *(9 am–7 pm Mon–Wed, Fri, Sat, 8 am–1 pm Sun)*. Famous *groups of sculptures* before the entrance, including a marble copy of Michelangelo's *David* (original is in the Galleria dell'Accademia; *8.30 am–6.50 pm Tue–Sat; 8.30 am–1.50 pm Sun; Via Ricasoli, 60*) and a copy of Donatello's *Judith and Holofernes* (original in palace). At the corner is the monumental *Neptune Fountain* by Ammanati (1563–75).

Ponte Vecchio (U/C5)

🜨 ⚔ This famous 14th-century bridge is home to shops and workshops: 36 goldsmiths and jewellery boutiques line both sides. The only bridge not destroyed during World War II, it is the oldest construction spanning the Arno (built in 1345) and is open only to pedestrians. The bridge is one of Florence's landmarks and really is a must.

S. Croce (U/E4–5)

Built for the Franciscan order between 1294–1385, this church contains the tombs of Michelangelo, Galileo Galilei, Niccolò Machiavelli, Gioacchino Rossini and other greats. Home to more artistic works than any other church in Florence, it is also famous for the wonderful 14th-century frescos found in the choir chapels. *Open in summer 8 am–6.30 pm daily, and in winter 8 am–12.30 pm and 3 pm–6 pm daily*

S. Lorenzo (U/C2)

This complex of buildings includes the Medici burial chapels and the Cappella dei Principe *(Chapel of the Princes , which is decorated lavishly with semi-precious stones. (Open 8.30 am–4 pm Tue, Thu and Fri, 8.30 am–1.50 pm Sat–Mon and Wed)* This church also includes the *Biblioteca Medicea Laurenziana.*

S. Maria del Carmine (U/A5)

The highlight of this church on the left bank of the Arno is the Brancacci Chapel with its cycle of frescos, *The Life of St. Peter.* These frescos are considered to be some of the most imposing and interesting examples of European Renaissance art. They were started in 1423–28 by Masolino da Panicale and Masaccio and completed in 1483 by Filippo Lippi. *Open 10 am –5 pm Wed–Sat, 1–5 pm Sun*

S. Maria Novella (U/B2)

Built for the Dominican order from 1246–1360 and mentioned by Boccaccio in his epic work

Decameron, it is one of the most beautiful churches in Florence. Its façade is of green and white marble and it is home to particularly impressive cycles of frescos. *Open 9 am–2 pm Mon–Thu, 9 am–2 pm Sat, and 8 am–1 pm Sun*

S. Miniato al Monte (O)

A gem of Romanesque-Florentine architecture high on a hill overlooking the left bank of the Arno. The nave of this basilica has splendid marble mosaic floor panels, an intricately carved marble pulpit and the *Cappella del Crocifisso* completed by Michelozzo in 1448. From ⇖ the stone steps there is a tremendous panoramic view! *Open 8 am–12 midday and 2 pm–7 pm daily in summer and 2.30 pm–6 pm daily in winter*

The Uffizi (U/C-D4-5)

★ In the 39 rooms of the upper floor the Uffizi houses one of the most significant art collections in the world. *Open 8.30 am–6.50 pm Tue–Sat and 8.30 am–1.50 pm Sun, sometimes until 10 pm in August*

RESTAURANTS

The cheapest – and very good – are near the markets, the finest and most expensive is the *Enoteca Pinchiorri (**U/E4**; Closed Mon and Wed lunch and Sun; Via Ghibellina, 87; Tel. 055 24 27 77; Category 1)*. Small but exquisite, *Cantinetta Antinori (**U/B3**, Closed Sat and Sun; Piazza Antinori; Tel. 055 29 22 34; Category 1–2)* and *Il Cibreo (**U/F4**; Closed Sun and Mon; Via dei Macci, 118r; Tel. 05 52 34 11 00; Category 2)*; quintessentially Florentine *Coco Lezzone (**U/B4**; Closed Sun; Via del Parioncino, 26r; Tel.*

055 28 71 78; Category 2) and *Il Latini (**U/B3**; closed Mon; Via Palchetti, 6r; Tel. 055 21 09 16; Category 3)*

SHOPPING

The most elegant shopping streets with Italy's top designers are ❖ *Via Tornabuoni (**U/C3-4**)* and *Via della Vigna Nuova (**U/B4**)*. The area around the Duomo and the ❖ ⚡ *Mercato S. Lorenzo (**U/C2**; Open 8 am –7 pm Mon–Sat)* adjacent to the church of the same name are not only good for window shopping. The *Mercato Centrale (**U/C2**; Open 7 am–2 pm Mon–Sat, and in winter also 4–8 pm Sat)* right next door provides an array of visual and culinary delights.

ACCOMMODATION

Alessandra (U/C4)

Friendly pensione on the upper floors of an old palace; ⇖ rooms 11, 20 and 21 have a view of the river. *25 rooms; Borgo SS. Apostoli, 17; Tel. 055 28 34 38; Fax 055 21 06 19; Category 3*

Croce di Malta (U/B3)

Near station, lovely courtyard, pool and restaurant. Suitable for the disabled. *83 rooms; Via della Scala, 7; Tel. 055 21 83 51; Fax 055 28 71 21; Category 1*

Helvetia & Bristol (U/C3)

Old English atmosphere in city centre. *52 rooms; Via dei Pescioni, 2; Tel. 055 28 78 14; Fax 055 28 83 53; Category 1*

Lungarno (U/B5)

Modern, comfortable establishment in Oltrarno between Ponte

Vecchio and Ponte S. Trinità. Garage. *66 rooms; Borgo S. Iacopo, 14; Tel. 055 26 42 11; Fax 055 26 84 37; Category 1*

Malaspina (**U/C1**)
Traditional, quiet city hotel. *31 rooms; Piazza dell'Indipendenza, 24; Tel. 055 48 98 69; Fax 055 47 48 09; Category 2*

Morandi alla Crocetta (**U/E2**)
Suitable for families; friendly service. A small, very pleasant establishment. *10 rooms; Via Laura, 50; Tel. 05 52 34 47 47; Fax 05 52 48 09 54; Category 2*

ENTERTAINMENT

During the winter season the *Teatro della Pergola* (**U/F3**; *Tel. 05 52 47 96 51)* and the Opera House *Teatro Comunale* (**O**; *Tel. 055 21 11 58)* regularly have performances and in *Stazione Leopolda* (**O**) there is experimental theatre and performances. There is always something interesting happening in the former prison *Le Murate* (**U/F3**; *Open daily from 10 pm)*. The places to meet and chat with many young people are the ≵ bistro cafés, serving snacks inside and outside on the street. At the time of writing the most popular were *La Dolce Vita* (**U/A4–5**; *Closed Mon; Piazza del Carmine), La Cabiria* (**U/A–B5**; *Closed Tue; Piazza S. Spirito), Il Caffè* (**U/B6**; *Open daily; Piazza Pitti, 9r)* and *Du Monde* (**U/E6**; *Closed Mon; Via S. Niccolò, 103r)*. The most frequented disco in Florence is *Meccanò* at the entrance to Cascine Park (**O**; *Closed Sun and Mon)*, and also *Central Park* (**O**) during the summer months, a huge open air disco at the end of the park. Another popular spot is the hard rock disco *Tenax*, on the edge of the city towards the airport (**O**; *10 pm– 3 am Thu–Sat)* and two disco pubs in the city centre, *Maramao* at Mercato S. Ambrogio (**U/F4**; *Open daily 5 pm–2 am)* and *Yab* near the Piazza della Repubblica (**U/C4**; *Closed Tue)*.

Detailed information about the city can be found in the MARCO POLO guide *Florence*.

Hotel and restaurant prices

Hotels
Category 1: above L250,000
Category 2: L120–250,000
Category 3: below L120,000
The prices are for a double room without breakfast.
Prices for accommodation vary greatly between seasons and areas: In summer a double room in Florence or on the coast can cost three times as much as the same room elsewhere in the region.

Restaurants
Category 1: above L80,000
Category 2: L40,000–80,000
Category 3: below L40,000
These prices are for a typical, local fixed menu including bread, cover charge and water. Indulging in expensive beverages can increase the cost – sometimes considerably.

Abbreviations
S. San/Sant(a)/Sant(o)

And the soul lies in Siena

Medieval towns and cities in the idyllic countryside are ideal for culture and relaxation

Siena, the provincial capital, is situated in the heart of Tuscany, which is bounded by Monte Amiata to the south-east, the Chianti region to the north, and the Province of Arezzo, with its historically significant hinterland to the east. While the ruby-red Chianti Classico is produced from grapes nurtured in the soil of the Chianti foothills, the area's best known wine, the Brunello di Montalcino, is a product of the red earth in the province's south, the *Terra di Siena*. The road to Asciano passes through the Crete region, a landscape of fascinating round clay hillocks eroded of topsoil by heavy rains over the centuries.

SIENA

☛ **City Map on page 36**

(122/B–C6) ★ Siena (pop. 57,000) is built on a series of ridges and owes its wealth to the lush countryside supporting the vineyards and olive groves which surround it.

Siena's Piazza del Campo: for many, Italy's most beautiful square

Siena has retained its medieval Gothic appearance. This is immediately apparent whether you follow the narrow streets and alleyways up to the Duomo or down to the shell-shaped town hall square, *Il Campo*. It is also evident from the numerous constricted stairways, delicate arches, sleepy squares, and typical red clay houses.

Along the three main arterial streets – Via di Città, Banchi di Sopra and Banchi di Sotto, which extend radially along the ridges to the Piazza del Campo – are the imposing palaces of the nobility and the city's more elegant shops. As the entire inner city area of Siena has been free of cars since 1959, a stroll along these level streets can be enjoyed by those who may be otherwise daunted by its steep narrow alleyways. The highest point of the city (365 m) is occupied by the majestic black and white marble Gothic Duomo. Facing it on a hill to the north-west is the massive brick basilica of S. Domenico. The church of S. Francesco is situated in an equally domineering position to the north-east. Siena has a 700-year-

MARCO POLO SELECTION: THE HEART OF TUSCANY

1 Abbazia S. Galgano
Summer concerts in a Gothic church nave flooded with sunlight (page 45)

2 S. Francesco in Arezzo
Frescos by Piero della Francesca (page 49)

3 Volterra
The medieval silhouette of the former Etruscan Lukomonie Velathri dominates this beautiful yet harsh landscape (page 44)

4 Chianti
Wooded hills, sprawling vineyards, fortresses and castles (page 40)

5 San Gimignano
An enchanting medieval city in beautiful and undulating countryside (page 42)

6 Siena
The Duomo is a marvel of Tuscan Gothic architecture, the city a medieval gem, the Palio, the largest festival in Italy (page 33)

old university and one of the most famous schools of music in all of Italy, the Accademia Chigiana.

The origins of Siena are unclear. The only thing that is certain is that there was a Roman colony by the name of Sena Julia. As a medieval ally of the Holy Roman Emperor, Siena was at war with papal Florence until 1555. On 17 April of that year the Sienese were finally vanquished after bloody battles and internal revolts. In 1559 the city became subject to the rule of the Medici duke, Cosimo I, and from that time on, destined to share Tuscany's fate. In 1859 Siena became the first Tuscan city to join the newly established state of Italy. Trade in agricultural products and more recently the flourishing tourist industry are the city's primary sources of income.

SIGHTS

Il Campo

❂ ♟ Cafés and restaurants occupying the ground floors of Gothic palaces encircle the shell-shaped square. Its herring-bone patterned, red brick paving is dissected by white strips of calcareous tuff, which appear to run together at the lowest point of the steeply-inclined square, directly before the Palazzo Pubblico. At the highest point there is the Fonte Gaia, the fountain designed by Jacapo della Quercia in 1412. The original reliefs are on view in the Palazzo Pubblico. What is arguably the most beautiful square in Italy has been the secular focal point of Siena since the early Middle Ages. Petitions for referendums have been presented here and tournaments or competitions held, such as the famous Palio delle

Contrade horse race held twice a year.

Duomo Nuovo

During the early 14th century, at the time Siena was enjoying its wealthiest period, the Council of Nine (municipal governing body comprising nine rich merchants) decided to enlarge the Duomo. The design was such that the previous cathedral (Duomo S. Maria) was to constitute only the transept of the new, massive edifice and the space between the south wall and the high arch was to become the nave. Building began in 1339, but work ceased in 1348 after the plague had decimated two-thirds of the population.

Closing the three right-hand arcades of the side aisle of the unfinished nave created the premises for the *Museo dell'Opera Metropolitana* (Duomo museum). It was established in 1870 and includes marble sculptures by Giovanni da Pisano and important paintings of the Sienese School by Simone Martini, Tad-

deo di Bartolo, Ambrogio Lorenzetti etc. The major treasure is, however, the renowned *Maestà* (1308–11) by Duccio da Buoninsegna. From the museum it is easy to climb the ❧ *façade* of the partially-completed cathedral in order to enjoy the spectacular 360-degree view! *Open daily: 15 March – 30 Sept 9 am–7.30 pm; Oct 9 am–6 pm; Nov – 14 March 9 am–1.30 pm*

Duomo S. Maria

Giovanni Pisano's façade is reminscent of a large French cathedral. The breathtaking interior is decorated with black and white marble stripes, the city's colours. The carved choir stalls and the circular glass window above the choir, designed by Duccio da Buoninsegna at the close of the 13th century, are also splendid. Mounted on nine pillars, the marble and porphyry pulpit (1266–68) with its realistically carved panels is the combined effort of Nicola Pisano, his son Giovanni, and Arnolfo Cambio. The cathedral is also unique by virtue of its marble floor, which is divided into 56 sections of varying dimensions, depicting sibyls and biblical scenes. The earliest representations, from the beginning of the 15th century, were carved into the marble. The grooves were then filled with tar. The later ones have been inlaid using marble of numerous colours. In the left-hand aisle is the entrance to the *Libreria Piccolomini*, erected by Francesco Todeschini Piccolomini, later to become Pope Pius III, to commemorate his uncle, Pope Pius II, and to house his collection of manuscripts.

Black and white, the colours of Siena, also dominate the Duomo

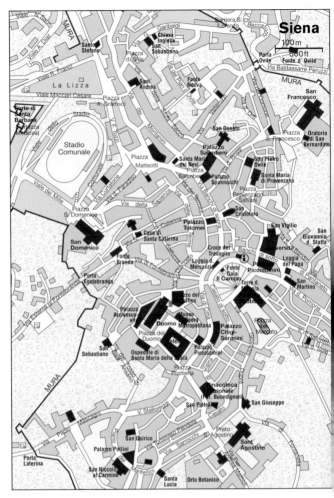

The frescos by Pinturicchio depict scenes from the life of Pius II. Behind the cathedral one finds the *S. Giovanni Baptistery* (1316), likewise with frescos by Pinturicchio and a hexagonal baptismal font with gilded bronze reliefs by Donatello, Jacopo della Quercia etc. *Open daily: Mid March–Oct 9 am–* *7.30 pm; Nov–mid March 10 am–1 pm and 2.30 pm–5 pm; Piazza del Duomo/Piazza S. Giovanni*

Forte di S. Barbara

〰️⊛⚘☖ From the gardens of the former Medici fortress there is a superb view of the old city, which is situated next to it. *Piazza La Lizza*

Palaces

The most memorable palaces in Siena are the *Palazzo Piccolomini delle Papesse*, built by Rosellino for Pius II between 1460–65 and one of the few Renaissance palaces in a largely Gothic city *(Via di Città, 126)*, and the *Palazzo Salimbeni* from the 14th century, with the *Palazzi Spannocchi* (right) and *Tantucci* (left) flanking it. The latter is the headquarters of the oldest surviving bank in the world, the Monte dei Paschi di Siena, which was founded in 1472. The bank's archives, kept intact since the bank opened, may be viewed by appointment *(Tel. 05 77 29 00 00). Piazza Salimbeni*

Palazzo Chigi-Saracini

Begun in the 12th century, this palace is considered by some to be the most beautiful in the city. It features a tower with battlements and three-piece Sienese windows. It houses the Accademia Musicale Chigiana and its courtyard is usually filled with the sound of orchestral tones. The palace maintains an extensive library and a collection of paintings, as well as a Baroque concert hall seating 350 people. You can receive information about Siena's Music Festival at the *Accademia Musicale Chigiana; Via di Città, 89, 53100 Siena; Tel. 057 74 61 52; Fax 05 77 28 81 24.*

Palazzo Pubblico and Museo Civico

The palace (which is also known as *Palazzo Comunale*) was built as the city's town hall between 1268 and 1342. The grand masters of the Sienese School were commissioned with providing its decoration. The most significant frescos can be seen in the rooms on the second floor, where the *Museo Civico* is housed: the two frescos comprising the *Allegory of Good and Bad Government* by Ambrogio Lorenzetti (1337) are in the *Sala della Pace* (unfortunately the fresco depicting *Bad Government* is badly damaged). The spacious *Sala del Mappamondo* contains the *Maestà* by Simone Martini and the large fresco *Guidoriccio* (1328). The 88 m tower, the ↘ Torre del Mangia, was constructed between 1338–48 and offers the best view over the city and the surrounding hills. The climb is arduous but worthwhile. At the base of the tower is the *Cappella di Piazza*, built as a loggia in 1352. *Opening times are seasonal: Palazzo Pubblico and Torre del Mangia from 9.30/ 10 am–5/6.30 pm Mon–Sat; 9.30 am–1.30 pm Sun; Piazza del Campo*

S. Agostino

↘ The Augustine church which was erected in 1258 houses three extremely valuable and impressive paintings: *Crucifixion* by Pietro Perugino, *Madonna* by Ambrogio Lorenzetti and *Three Wise Men* by Giovanni Sodoma. There is also a wonderful view from here. *Prato di S. Agostino*

S. Domenico

↘ From the forecourt of this brick basilica, there is also a fine view over the city. Although construction began in 1226, it was continually extended until 1465. The barn-like nave holds frescos by Sodoma, depicting scenes from the life of St. Catherine of Siena. Her head can be viewed in the tabernacle on the high altar. *Open daily 9 am–12.30 pm and 3.30 pm–6 pm; Piazza S. Domenico*

S. Francesco

❧ The climb up to this church is rewarded by being able to view the exquisite frescos by Ambrogio Lorenzetti. The *Oratorium S. Bernardino* was erected next to the church in the 15th century on this very spot from where St. Bernhard preached. Beautiful frescos by Sodoma and Beccafumi. *Piazza S. Francesco*

MUSEUMS

All national and municipal museums in Siena are closed on 1 January, 1 May and 25 December.

Accademia dei Fisiocritici

Includes the *Museo Geomineralogico*, the *Museo Paleontologico* and the *Museo Zoologico*. These museums are located in the former Camaldoli monastery. Even for the less scientifically minded the museum complex should prove interesting. Next to the monastery one finds the *Orto Botanico*, the university's botanical garden, which was established in 1588 and covers roughly two hectares. It has a particularly large collection of various species. *Museums: Open 9 am–1 pm and 3 pm–6 pm Mon–Fri, Thu afternoon; Closed Sat and Sun; Piazza S. Agostino, 4. Garden: 8 am–5 pm Mon–Fri, 8 am–12 midday Sat; Via Pier Andrea Mattioli, 4*

Archivio di Stato and Museo delle Tavole di Biccherna

The national archives are housed in the Palazzo Piccolomini, which was built in 1469 by Bernardo Rossellino. They encompass approximately 62,000 parchments and about 140,000 historic bundles of files documenting the history of the city. The incorporated Museo delle Tavole di Biccherna contains 105 hand-painted, wooden book covers which were used to bind the public expenditure documents until the 18th century. Their designs were conceived by the famous artists of each era. *Open 9 am–1 pm Mon–Sat; Closed 1 and 16 Aug; Banchi di Sotto, 52*

Museo Archeologico Nazionale

The archeological museum was established in 1996 in one of the oldest hospitals in the world (early 13th century), the *Spedale S. Maria della Scala. Open 9 am–2 pm Mon–Sat, 9 am–1 pm Sun; Closed every 2nd and 4th Sunday of month; Piazza Duomo*

Museo della Società di Esecutori di Pie Disposizioni

A small museum where Sienese masterpieces by artists from Duccio da Buoninsegna to Rutilio Manetti can be viewed in peace. *Open only by appointment 9 am–12 midday Mon–Fri, also 3 pm–5 pm Tue and Thu; Tel. 05 77 28 43 00; Via Roma, 71*

Pinacoteca Nazionale and Collezione Spannocchi

Housed in the Palazzo Buonsignori is one of the most important museums in Tuscany. Its 700 or more painted panels give an uninterrupted representation of Sienese painting from the 12th to the 16th centuries. The Spannocchi Collection, on the other hand, has paintings from northern Europe. *Open 9 am–7 pm Tue–Sat, 8 am–1 pm Sun; 8.30 am–1.30 pm Mon; Via S. Pietro, 29*

Santuario Cateriniano

❖ Still in its original Gothic state, this is the house where Caterina Benincasa (1347–1380) was born. The daughter of a dyer, she was persuaded by Pope Gregor XI to return from Avignon to Rome in 1377. The living area has several devotional rooms decorated with valuable art works. *Open daily 9 am– 12.30 pm and 3.30 pm (Summer 2.30 pm)–6 pm; Costa di S. Antonio*

RESTAURANTS

Antica Trattoria Botteganova

Cosy family-run business, good food. *Closed Monday; Strada Chiantigiana, 29; Tel. 05 77 28 42 30; Category 2*

Buca S. Pietro

⚘ Only a few yards from the Campo, this quaint establishment offers Tuscan specialties. *Closed Sun; Vicolo S. Pietro, 4; Tel. 057 74 01 3 9; Category 2*

Il Campo

Traditional dishes, elegant. *Closed Tue; Piazza del Campo, 50; Tel. 05 77 28 07 25; Category 2*

Il Giuggiolo

The food served here is excellent, especially the hearty fare typical of the Tuscan countryside. *Closed Wed; Via Massetana, 30; Tel. 05 77 28 42 95; Category 2*

Il Grattacielo

Small student eatery offering tasty snacks and good meals – but only from 8 am–2 pm and from 5 pm–8 pm. *Closed Sun; Via di Salicotto, 7; Category 3*

Osteria Le Logge

The best known culinary establishment in Siena. *Closed Sun; Via del Porrione, 33; Tel. 057 74 80 13, Category 2*

Pizzeria San Martino

For those who find Le Logge too expensive or too full, just a few buildings along. *Closed Sun; Via del Porrione, 64; Category 3*

SHOPPING

You should buy some *panforte* (dense dark cake spiced with cloves and cinnamon), *ricciarelli* (marzipan biscuits), ceramics and wine from the area around Siena.

Antica Drogheria Manganelli

❖ Sweets sold here since 1879. *Via di Città, 71–73*

Enoteca Italica Permanente

Italy's largest wine merchant; wine tasting and direct shipment possible. *Open daily 12 midday –12.30/1 am; Fortezza Medicea; Tel. 05 77 28 84 97*

ACCOMMODATION

In winter Siena usually offers a package with cheaper accommodation and some additional discounts within the province. Information can be obtained from: *Siena Hotels Promotion; Piazza S. Domenico; Tel. 05 77 28 80 84; Fax 05 77 28 02 90*

Certosa di Maggiano

A former monastery set in parklands with a pool. Located on the edge of town and has facilities for the disabled. *15 rooms and suites; Strada di Certosa, 82; Tel. 05 77 28 81 80; Fax 05 77 28 81 89; Category 1*

Garden

⬧⬧ Wonderful view of Siena, friendly service, garden and swimming pool. Facilities for the disabled. *136 rooms; Via Custoza, 2; Tel. 057 74 70 56; Fax 057 74 60 50; Category 1–2*

Ostello Il Guidoriccio

This friendly youth hostel is at the northern end of the town. Bus service to town centre. *Via Fiorentina, 89; Tel. 057 75 22 12; Fax 057 75 61 72*

Palazzo Ravizza

Stylish atmosphere in a former palace right in town centre. Hotel garage. *30 rooms; Pian dei Mantellini, 34; Tel. 05 77 28 04 62; Fax 05 77 27 13 70; Category 2*

Park Hotel

⬧⬧ Luxury and space in a villa at the edge of town; pool and tennis courts. Facilities for the disabled. *69 rooms; Via Marciano, 16; Tel. 057 74 48 03; Fax 057 74 90 20; Category 1*

Piccolo Hotel Il Palio

Located centrally and inexpensive, ideal for tours of the town. Facilities for the disabled. *26 rooms; Piazza del Sale, 19; Tel. 05 77 28 11 31; Fax 05 77 28 11 42; Category 3*

Villa Scacciapensieri

⬧⬧ Located at the northern edge of town, with pool, tennis court and terrace. Facilities for the disabled. *29 rooms; Via di Scacciapensieri, 10; Tel. 057 74 14 41; Fax 05 77 27 08 54; Category 1*

Club Enoteca

A disco near the *enoteca. Fortezza Medicea; Tel. 05 77 28 54 66*

L'Officina

Cosy *birreria* featuring live music. *Closed Wed; Piazza del Sale, 3*

Porta Giustizia 11

Directly behind the Campo – candles and keyboards. *Open 9.30 pm–2 am Tue–Thu, 5 pm–2 am Fri–Sun; Via di Porta Giustizia, 11*

Via di Città, 43, 53100 Siena; Tel. 05 77 28 05 51; Fax 05 77 28 10 41

★ Due to its location between Florence and Siena, the Chianti region is an ideal area to enjoy a refreshing holiday 'between Art and Wine' – that's why we provide numerous tips regarding hotels and restaurants. There is a well-run youth hostel, the *Ostello del Chianti*, in *50028 Tavarnelle Val di Pesa; 60 beds; Via Roma, 137; Tel. 05 58 07 70 09; Fax 05 58 05 01 04.*

The best contact addresses for vineyard vacations can be obtained from *Le Stagioni del Chianti (Via di Campoli, 142, 50024 Mercatale; Tel. 055 82 14 81; Fax 055 82 14 49).* Picnics and excursions on foot or by mountain bike can be organized by Affresco *(Via de'Benci, 24, 50122 Firenze; Tel. 05 52 47 78 35;*

Fax 05 52 47 83 08), and those who would like to soar over the Chianti in a hot air balloon can contact *Idea Balloon (Via di Gualdo, 8, 50019 Sesto Fiorentino; Tel. 05 54 48 19 92 and 033 89 07 70 70)*. The flight lasts about one–and–a–half hours and costs L300,000 per person.

Castellina in Chianti (122/B3-4)

❧ Charming, medieval town in the Chianti hills. Situated on a hillside, the *Tenuta di Ricavo* is a tastefully restored group of old farmhouses with swimming pool and park. *(19 rooms with facilities for the disabled; Tel. 05 77 74 02 21; Fax 05 77 74 10 14; Closed Nov–April)*. Here and in the nearby *Villa Casalecchi (16 rooms; Tel. 05 77 74 02 40; Fax 05 77 74 11 11; Closed Nov–March)* you can enjoy a really relaxing holiday with all creature comforts. *Both Category 1*

Gaiole in Chianti (123/D3-4)

Gaiole is in a particularly pretty area and has two small Romanesque churches worth visiting *(Pieve di S. Marcellino* and *S. Pietro in Avenano)*. In the former Vallombrosano monastery, *Badia a Coltibuono* (11th century), one of the oldest vineyards, there is also a restaurant *(Tel. 05 77 74 94 24; Category 2)*. In the *Castello di Spaltenna* (also a former monastery from the 11th century) you can stay and dine superbly *(Closed Jan–March and Monday; 21 rooms; Tel. 05 77 74 94 83; Fax 05 77 74 92 69; Category 1)*. Ten km south of Gaiole, on the SS 484, one finds the formidable *Castello di Brolio,* surrounded by 200 hectares of vineyards. Castle and cellars can be viewed. *(Open daily 10 am–*

12 midday and 3 pm–5 pm, Sun to 6 pm).

Greve in Chianti (122/B2)

Capital city (pop. 11,000) of the Chianti, with its lovely market square surrounded by leafy passageways and with the hotel restaurant *Da Verrazzano (11 rooms; Tel. 055 85 31 89; Hotel closed in Feb; Restaurant closed Sun evening and Mon; Category 3)*. At the southern end of the Piazza you find the *Enoteca del Chianti Classico* serving local wines *(Tel. 055 58 32 97)*. In the first week of September the *Mostra Mercato Vino Chianti Classico* trade fair takes place. Greve also has the magnificent *Villa Vignamaggio* from the 15th century, with a beautiful park. It is here that Mona Lisa was born and captured on canvas by Leonardo da Vinci. There are guest rooms and apartments available for tourists on this old estate (wine and olive oil). *Cenobio di Villa Vignamaggio; Tel. 055 85 35 59; Fax 05 58 54 44 68; Category 1–2*

Impruneta (118/B5)

The church of *S. Maria* (11th century) is situated on Impruneta's broad square and features a fine portico from the 16th century and holds important art treasures. The city (pop. 15,000) is famous for its pottery works. The terracotta vases on the Piazza are from *Mario Mariani; Via Cappello, 29. Hotel Bellavista*, whose owner also loves to serve *spaghettata* on the terrace above the square, has simple and clean rooms. *(12 rooms; Tel. 05 52 01 10 83; Fax 05 52 31 39 29; Category 3)*. At Ristorante *I Cavallacci* you eat outside in summer and in the beautifully decorated rooms the rest of the year (*Open daily, Viale Aldo Moro, 3, Tel. 05 52 31 38 63; Category 2*).

Panzano in Chianti (122/B2)

From the forecourt of the Romanesque ☙ *Pieve S. Leolino* there is a wonderful view – and also from most rooms of Hotel *Villa Sangiovese* situated on the small village square, which can also be recommended for a brief visit (*Closed Christmas–Feb; 17 rooms; Tel. 055 85 24 61; Fax 055 85 24 63; Category 2*). Half-board is obligatory at *Villa Le Barone*, a country residence from the 16th century with a pretty park and swimming pool (*Closed Nov–March, 27 rooms; Tel. 055 85 26 21; Fax 055 85 22 77; Category 2*).

Radda in Chianti (122/C3)

Radda is one of the most enchanting towns in Chianti. The olive trees which encircle the medieval ☙ *Castello di Volpaia* at an altitude of 600 m, produce the best oil in the area and an excellent Chianti also comes from here. You can try both with a ham sandwich in the small *Osteria* (*Fattoria open daily 9 am–1 pm and 4 pm–7.30 pm; Osteria closed Fri; Tel. 05 77 73 80 66*). Stay over and dine in style at *Relais Vignale* (*Closed Dec–March and Thu; 26 rooms; Tel. 05 77 73 83 00; Fax 05 77 73 85 92; Facilities for the disabled; Category 1*). At *Fornace Campo al Sole* you can buy the large coveted clay pots (*orci*).

Ugolino (118/B5)

Along national highway 222, the 'Chiantigiana', 12 km south of Florence near Grassina, there is a very pretty *golf course* with 18 holes. Good *swimming pool (Tel. 05 52 30 10 09)*.

Monteriggioni (122/A5)

☙ Situated along the highway between Florence and Siena, the town rises up on a hill like a fortress. Monteriggioni has retained its medieval character; totally enclosed by a turreted city wall, you can only enter the village through either one of the two gates. On the village square you find the restaurant *Il Pozzo* (*Closed Sun evening and Mon; Tel. 05 77 30 41 27; Category 2*). Three kilometres away in *Abbadia Isola* there is the small but elegant *Antica Osteria La Leggenda dei Frati* (*Closed Mon; Tel. 05 77 30 12 22; Category 2*).

San Gimignano (121/E3–4)

★ The silhouette of the 'Manhattan of Tuscany', with its tall medieval towers reaching heights of 54 m, is clearly visible from quite a distance. The town (pop. 7,000) has become one of the main tourist destinations in the region, and during the holiday season the *Via S. Giovanni* leading to the cathedral square is correspondingly busy. If you head off into side alleys or up the hill behind the square you can enjoy some peace and quiet – and a wonderful view of the surrounding countryside at a number of spots. The town is entirely encircled by a wall, which has only five gates providing access to it. Medieval San Gimignano had up to 72 fortified and inhabited towers at any one time. The families of the Guelfs, who supported the Pope, and the Ghibel-

The towers of the nobility symbolize San Gimignano

lines, who owed their allegiance to the Emperor, fought against each other for decades. The respective winners then razed the losers' towers to the ground – only two can be climbed today ◈ (wonderful view!).

The *Piazza della Cisterna* is a well-balanced square, with a fountain, the Hotel La Cisterna and its restaurant ◈ *Le Terrazze*, which offers a panoramic view *(Closed Wed midday and Tue, 49 rooms; Tel. 05 77 94 03 28; Fax 05 77 94 20 80; Category 2)*. The *Piazza del Duomo* is directly adjacent. Inside the *Collegiata* (built in the 12th century and extended in the 15th century) there are exceptionally well-preserved fresco cycles by Barna da Siena, Taddeo di Bartolo, Lippo Memmi, Benozzo Gozzoli and Ghirlandaio (Cappella di S. Fina). The *Palazzo del Popolo*, with its heraldic decoration and lovely inner courtyard, is on the same square, as are the *Museo Civico* and the *Pinacoteca (Open

daily: March–Oct 9.30 am–7.30 pm; Nov–Feb 9.30 am–12.50 pm and 2.30–4.50 pm Tue–Sun)*, and also the *Palazzo del Podestà* and the *Palazzo della Propositura* (13th century). Every year in July and August on the steps of the basilica there are performances of the 'Estate Sangimignanese' concert and opera productions *(Information and tickets through Pro Loco, Piazza Duomo, 1, 53037 San Gimignano; Tel. 05 77 94 00 08; Fax 05 77 94 09 03)*. To the north, near the *Porta S. Matteo*, is the *S. Agostino* monastery (13th century). Inside the church there are very pretty frescos with images from the life of the saint by Benozzo Gozzoli.

The rooms at Hotel ◈ *Pescille*, 3 km away toward Castel San Gimignano, can be recommended and have wonderful views of the town; tennis court and swimming pool *(Closed Nov–Feb; 48 rooms; Tel. 05 77 94 01 86; Fax 05 77 94 31 65; Category 2)*. You can also stay in style

8 km to the west at *Casolare di Libbiano*, a small farmstead which has been tastefully extended. It is situated in a peaceful location and offers a swimming pool and half-board, the food being prepared using their own produce *(Closed Nov–Easter; Tel. and Fax 05 77 94 60 02; Category 2)*.

San Gimignano is also famous for the white wine grown in the area, the Vernaccia, which you can savour in the *trattorie* and restaurants in the town.

Volterra   (120/C5)

〰 ★ The road to this former Etruscan town, perched 555 m above sea level, is very windy and hilly. Over the millennia, rain and wind have transformed this tuff landscape into a strange and fascinating moonscape, with a myriad of *balze* (precipices). The untamed earth has claimed a number of inanimate victims over the last few decades: part of the Etruscan city wall, a monastery, and for the second time, the San Giusto church, which has been rebuilt yet again. This geological movement exposed unique remnants of the Villanova culture (10th–8th centuries B.C.), providing the town with a new tourist attraction.

The town, dominated today by the massive *Medici Fortress* (prison), was once known as Velathri and belonged to the Dodecapolis, the alliance formed by twelve of Etruria's most powerful towns. Remnants of the Etruscan town wall, the exceptionally well-preserved *Arco Etrusco* and a large collection of artefacts from that bygone era testify to its former wealth. The *Museo Guarnacci*

(Open daily: April–Oct 9 am–7 pm; Nov-March 9 am–2 pm; Closed 1 Jan and 25 Dec) holds over 600 urns and sarcophagi, all meticulously arranged and presented. Even with far less exquisite items this museum would still be well worth a visit! Apart from the realistically decorated coffins there are vases and jewellery – and the almost painfully thin bronze statue *Shadow of the Evening (Ombra della Sera)*, replicas of which are available everywhere in the town.

The Romans named the town Volaterrae – and left behind an *amphitheatre (Open daily: mid March–end of Oct 11 am–5 pm)*. But today Volterra (pop. 13,000) is dominated by its medieval edifices and palaces, its focal point being the fortress-like *Palazzo dei Priori* (town hall) from 1208. Facing it is the *Palazzo del Pretorio*, with its triple-arched *Loggia*. The *Palazzo Incontri* (15th century) is located on the corner. The *Duomo* (12th century) features a simple façade and an exquisite pulpit, as well as frescos and sculptures. The octagonal *Baptistery* (13th century) is often a venue for exhibitions. The *Museo Civico* and the *Pinacoteca* which displays important works by the Florentine School (particularly impressive is the *Deposition* by Rosso Fiorentino) are to be found in the *Palazzo Minucci Solaini* (Antonio da Sangallo the elder) *(Opening times same as Museo Guarnacci)*.

Volterra is the city of alabaster. Wherever you go the sound of grinding machines can be heard and the shops are filled with works of art made from this mineral gypsum. In the *Gallerie*

Agostiane, a former Augustine monastery, antique and modern alabaster pieces can be purchased. At *Rossi Alabastro*, in *Via del Mandorlo*, you can even have a go at working with alabaster yourself. The centrally located Hotel *San Lino (44 rooms; Via S. Lino, 26; Tel. 058 88 52 50; Fax 058 88 06 20; Category 2)* is very comfortable, while the youth hostel *(Ostello della Gioventù; Via del Poggetto; Tel. 058 88 55 77; Fax 05 88 87 88 07)* is cheaper. You can dine particularly well in the magnificently rustic *Ristorante Etruria* on *Piazza dei Priori (Closed Thu; Tel. 058 88 60 64; Category 2)*.

SOUTH OF SIENA

Abbazia di Monte Oliveto Maggiore   (125/E3)

↝ The abbot has written cordially that guests are welcome at the *Foresteria* of the 273-metre brick monastery complex (14th century) located in a pine forest *(Bookings: Tel. 05 77 70 70 17)*. No matter what, you should take a look at the *cloister*, which is decorated with 36 frescos by Luca Signorelli (1497) and Sodoma (1505) *(Open daily 9.15 am–12 midday and 3.15 pm–5 pm, and in summer to 5.45 pm)*. The 35-km trip from Siena via Asciano (SS 438) leads through the dramatically eroded *crete* landscape with its lunar appearance.

Abbazia di S. Galgano   (110/A4)

↝ The Gothic Cistercian abbey (about 1224) stands alone on a wide, verdant plain. Only the outer walls, the chapterhouse and parts of the cloisters remain. During the summer months

★ concerts are held in the sun-lit nave of the church (Information: *APT in Siena*). Just a few metres away on a hill is the small Romanesque church *Monte Siepi* with frescos by Ambrogio Lorenzetti *(Both open daily 8 am–12 midday and 2 pm–sunset)*. After a concert you can dine and then stay at a particularly delightful hotel, where you can swim in the Merse River. You can also enjoy excellent cuisine 15 km to the east near *S. Lorenzo a Merse* on the SS 223 (Siena–Grosseto) at *La Locanda del Ponte; 23 rooms; Tel. 05 77 75 71 08; Fax 05 77 75 71 10; Hotel Category 1; Restaurant Category 2*

Bagni di Petriolo   (124/B5)

❀ ⚱ On the SS223 from Siena to Grosseto one finds *thermal baths (Tel. 05 77 75 71 04)* with an ancient bath house. In winter you can also dive into the Farma River which is fed by the 43°C (110°F) cascades. Recuperate from your bathing experience by having a meal at the simple *Locanda Bagni di Petriolo (Tel. 05 77 75 70 97; Category 3)*.

Chianciano and Chianciano Terme   (111/D4)

↝ This medieval town is situated on a hill right on the Umbrian border (leave the car – narrow alleys). After those in Montecatini, these baths, which are set in a valley, are the most popular in Tuscany. Liver complaints are those most commonly treated at the modern spa facilities. Most hotels, some dating from the turn of the century, are located in the surrounding countryside. Information is available from the *APT (Viale Sabatini, 7,*

*53042 Chianciano; Tel. 057 86
3538; Fax .057 86 46 23).*

Chiusi (111/D5)

〰️ The Etruscan town of Cha-
mars, one of the 12 main settle-
ments in the Etruscan league in
the 6th and 7th centuries B.C.,
is built on a Travertine hill,
dominating the Chiana Valley.
The main attractions are the
Museo Archeologico Nazionale with
its large collection of crema-
tion urns, vases decorated with
black figures, and Bucchero
ware, burnished to resemble
bronze *(Open 9 am–1.45 pm
Tue–Sat, 9 am–12.45 pm Sun; Via
Porsenna, 93)* and the *tombs* with
rich fresco decorations found in

Blooming gorse near Montalcino

the surrounding area. If you're
interested in receiving expert
guidance when visiting them
you can contact the custodian of
the museum *(Tel. 057 82 01 77).*
Outstanding meals and premium wines can be had at
Ristorante Zaira. Its wine cellar is
well worth a visit *(Closed Monday;
Via Arunte, 12; Tel. 057 82 02 60;
Category 2).* You can stay overnight and dine well while enjoying a view of Lago di Chiusi
at *La Fattoria (8 rooms; Tel. 057
82 14 07; Fax 057 82 06 44;
Category 3).*

Montalcino (125/D5)

〰️ Montalcino (pop. 5,000) is
noted for a *fortress* from the 14th
century *(Open 9 am–1 pm and
2.30 pm–8 pm Tue–Sun; Winter
2 pm–6 pm; Summer also open
Mon).* The Brunello produced in
the world-famous town is
among the best red wine in
Italy. You can sample a number
of Brunello wines and have a
snack in the fortress *Enoteca,* or

you can also wine and dine in
style at the *Cucina di Edgardo
(Closed Wed;Tel. and Fax 05 77 84
82 32; Category 2).*

Comfortable rooms are available at the fine Hotel-Ristorante
*Il Giglio (Closed Tue, 12 rooms; Tel.
and Fax 05 77 84 81 67; Category
3).* The menu at the tavern in the
nearby *Fattoria dei Barbi* is a real
piece of art. Don't be put off by
the 5-km drive to this vineyard
– the cellars alone are worth the
trip *(Closed Wed; Tel. 05 77 84 82
77; Category 2).*

In a small valley 10 km south
there is one of the most impressive Romanesque churches in
Italy, the *S. Antimo* Benedictine
abbey, which according to legend was founded by Charles the
Great. Today all that remains of
the monastery, which was disbanded in 1492, is the massive
basilica of honey-coloured travertine (12th century), the *refectory,* and the *chapterhouse (Open
10.30 am–12.30 pm and 3–6.30 pm*

Mon–Sat; 9.30–10.45 pm and 3 pm–6 pm Sun).

Monte Amiata (110/C5)

⬧⬦ The massive volcanic cone of Monte Amiata rises up to reach an altitude of 1738 m above the surrounding hills of southern Tuscany. Its slopes are blanketed with wild chestnut and oak forests. In the summer months the terrain is ideal for walking tours and there are well-marked trails. Detailed information is available from *Amiata Trekking (Piazza Gramsci, 8, 53021 Abbadia S. Salvatore; Tel. 05 77 77 77 51).*

The northern slopes are especially suitable for pursuing winter sports well into spring. There are numerous places to stay in the mountain villages. A trip through the unadulterated mountain countryside is always a great experience and offers magnificent views. The towns of *Abbadia S. Salvatore* (Benedictine monastery), *Arcidosso* (fortress), *Piancastagnaia* (Rocca Aldobrandesca) and *Santa Fiora*, where you can partake of a hearty meal at *Ristorante Il Barilotto (Closed Wed; Via Carolina, 24; Tel. 05 64 97 70 89; Category 2–3)*, are particularly worth a visit.

Montepulciano (110/C4)

⬧⬦ Known to wine connoisseurs the world over, this fortified town (pop. 14,000) is located on a hilly ridge. It is here that the most celebrated wine in Tuscany, the Vino Nobile, is produced. Monte Policiano, as it was named by the Romans, was probably established back in Etruscan times. Its heyday was in the 15th and 16th centuries, and its many palaces testify to the former wealth of the town. The streets climb up to the elegant *Piazza Grande*, bounded by the medieval *Palazzo del Capitano del Popolo* (12th century), the *Palazzi Tarugi* and *Contucci* (both by Andrea da Sangallo, 16th century), the *Palazzo Comunale* (Michelozzo, 1440), and the *Duomo* (17th century), which has an impressive altar by Andrea della Robbia. You can dine well and stay overnight at *Il Marzocco (16 rooms; Tel. 05 78 75 72 62; Fax 05 78 75 75 30; Category 3)*. Only a few kilometres to the south-west is the pilgrim church of *S. Biagio* (16th century) with its beautiful Canonica (Antonio da Sangallo).

Monticchiello (110/C4)

This small mountain village on the verge of the Crete district and to the southeast of Pienza is very special. In winter the farmers and their families spend their non-working hours rehearsing their self-penned scripts, which deal with the daily trials and tribulations of village life. And in July and August they tread the boards as actors in their own production on the tiny village square. The so-called ✦✝ *Teatro Poverto di Monticchiello* has received international acclaim *(Tel. 05 78 75 51 18)*.

Pienza (125/F5)

A must for Renaissance buffs! At the beginning of the 15th century Pope Pius II, Enea Silvio Piccolomini, commissioned the architects Leon Battista Alberti and Bernardo Gambarelli, a.k.a. Rossellino, to reconstruct Corsignano, his birthplace, as an ideal Renaissance town. They didn't manage to complete their work before his death in 1464, but the heart of the town , the *Piazza Piccolomini*, was finished. This brick-paved quadrangle is bounded by the *Duomo*, the *Palazzi Ammanati* and *Vescovile* and the reconstructed *judicial palace*. The rear of the *Palazzo Piccolomini*, which dominates the square, opens out over the Orcia Valley and Monte Amiata – a magnificent view, which can be enjoyed from the ✎ *Museo Palazzo Piccolomini (9 am–12 midday and 3 pm–5 pm Tue–Sun).* You should also try the *pecorino* (sheep's milk cheese), available through out the entire year, and all other local culinary titbits at the *Bottega del Naturalista* at *Corso Rossellino, 16.* Just a few paces further on, the cells in one of monasteries from the 15th century have been tastefully renovated to create a 48-room hotel *(Il Chiostro di Pienza; Tel. 05 78 74 84 00; Fax 05 78 74 84 40; Category 2).* One of the best restaurants in southern Tuscany, the *Fattoria La Chiusa* is to be found in *Montefollonico*, 10 km to the north-east, and in addition to excellent meals it offers 12 gorgeous rooms in an adjacent building *(Closed Tue; Tel. 05 77 66 96 68; Fax 05 77 66 95 93; Category 1)*

S. Quirico d'Orcia   (125/E–F5)

A typically Sienese town (pop. 2,000) with windy streets and brick towers. The huge *Palazzo Chigi* (17th century) and the Orti Leonini, an extensive garden in 16th-century style, are worth visiting. In picturesque *Bagno Vignoni*, 5 km south, there is a huge, steaming thermal pool (51°C/124°F) in the centre of the town, and a hotel-restaurant with facilities for the disabled, set in a pretty spot. *(Posta Marcucci; 46 rooms; Tel.* 05 77 88 71 12; Fax 05 77 88 71 19; Category 2).

AREZZO

(111/D2) Arezzo's (pop. 92,000) position in a valley between Arno and Tiber is economically advantageous, but not visually spectacular. You have to drive through the outer suburbs of this expanding city and press forward into the medieval city centre (pedestrian zone) in order to really appreciate its beauty. As early as 600 B.C. Arezzo was an important centre and by the 3rd century B.C. one of the major cities in the Etruscan league. In 88 B.C. the Romans granted civil rights to this town on the Via Cassia, known then as Arretium. The city developed into a gold-processing and pottery centre (the coral-coloured Aretino pottery was in great demand throughout the entire Roman Empire), with a temple, thermal baths and a theatre; today only the ruins of the amphitheatre provide an indication of its former prosperity. Caio Cilnio Mecenate, who later became advisor to Emperor Octavius and a major patron of the arts, was probably born here in 68 B.C. Guido of Arezzo, who introduced musical notation and scales to European music, also lived here from 990–1050 A.D. In the Middle Ages Ghibelline Arezzo was in constant conflict with Guelf Florence and in 1384 the city finally lost to its superior rivals.

The ensuing years of peace saw many of those churches and buildings constructed, which have given Arezzo the art-historical significance it enjoys today.

In 1304 the major poet and Humanist Francesco Petrarca was born in Arezzo. From 1453 trough 1464 a painter named Piero, from the town of Sansepolcro, worked in the city and adorned the main chapel of S. Francesco church with frescos, considered to be among the most beautiful in the world; modern art historians know this artist as Piero della Francesca. The following centuries saw the town subside into virtual insignificance and it only experienced an economic revival when the Florence–Rome railway track was built in 1866.

SIGHTS

Duomo S. Donato

Starting in the 13th century, the people of Arezzo worked on their sandstone basilica with its exquisite stained-glass windows (16th century) for 300 years. The high altar, a joint project by Arezzo's artists (14th century), has a shrine containing the bones of St. Donatus. In the left-hand aisle there is a fresco by Piero della Francescas from 1465, depicting Mary Magdalene. *Piazza del Duomo*

Palazzo dei Priori

The tin-crowned palace from the 13th century with its massive ❧ tower (1337), which you can climb, is located opposite the cathedral. The palace has been the seat of the town's administration since its construction. Beautiful inner courtyard. *Piazza della Libertà*

Piazza Grande

❖ Since Roman times this irregular, slightly sloping square has been both the town's focal point and market square. On its western side is the apse of *Pieve S. Maria,* the *Palazzo del Tribunale* from the 17th century with its parapet and a projecting external stairway, and the *Palazzo della Fraternità*, built between 1375 and 1460 by Bernardo Rossellino and Giuliano da Settignano. The *tower* was set in place in 1552. A feature of the medieval buildings on the eastern and southern sides of the square is the impressive towers. The northern side of the square is defined by the *Palazzo delle Logge*. This palace, designed in 1573 by Giorgio Vasari, completely destroys the architectural balance of the medieval square. It houses restaurants, ice-cream parlours and workshops in its arcades.

S. Domenico

The most treasured piece in this simple church (14th century) on the northern outskirts of the city is a large wooden cross suspended above the high altar, an early work by Cimabue (about 1265). Remnants of frescos and the Gothic Dragondelli Chapel are found in the single nave which features a beautiful wooden ceiling. A Romanesque portal decorates the undressed stone façade. *Piazza S. Domenico*

S. Francesco

★ The façade of this massive church has never been completed. Construction began in the second half of the 13th century, but the nave (53 x 17 m) was remodelled in the austere Tuscan-Gothic style of Franciscan churches in the 14th century. Above the high altar there is a painted wooden crucifix from the School of Cimabue (13th century) and in the left-hand chapel a beautiful monumental tomb (mid-15th century). The basilica's major attraction is its main choir, decorated with the wonderful frescos, *The Legend of the True Cross*, painted by Piero della Francesca in the years between 1453 and 1464. Restoration of the frescos, which has been in progress for years, is meant to be finished in the near future. The completed works on the left-hand side of the main chapel can be viewed at close quarters from a raised walkway. *30-minute guided tours: 9 am–1 pm and 3 pm–5.30 pm Mon–Sat, 3 pm–5.30 pm Sun only; Piazza S. Francesco*

S. Maria delle Grazie
A small Gothic church at the south-east end of the town with an elegant pillared entrance hall by Benedetto da Maiano (about 1470). The nave has a beautiful marble altar by Andrea della Robbia with a fresco of the Madonna by Parri di Spinello. *Viale Mecenate*

S. Maria della Pieve
The curious bell tower, *campanile delle cento buche* (tower of a hundred holes), gains its name from its 40 Romanesque double-arched windows. The façade of this church, erected in 1140 on the site of a 10th-century church, consists of three rows of sandstone columns in Pisan Romanesque style. On the high altar there is a beautiful polyptych by Pietro Lorenzetti from 1320. The crypt is also impressive. *Corso Italia*

MUSEUMS

Casa del Vasari
The home of Giorgio Vasari (1511–1574), painter and favourite architect of the Medici grand dukes. It is a classic example of a residence belonging to one of the upper middle-class citizens with artistic taste in the Cinquecento (16th century). Archive and museum. *Open daily 9 am–7 pm; Via XX Settembre, 55*

Museo Archeologico Statale Gaio Cilnio Mecenate
The former Olivetane monastery of S. Bernardo was built on the ruins of a Roman amphitheatre, and today it houses an exhibition of important archeological artefacts. Of particular interest is the large collection of Roman Aretine pottery, the *vasi corallini. Open 9 am–2 pm Tue–Sat, 9 am–1 pm Sun; Via Margaritone, 10*

Museo del Duomo
The museum contains a rich collection of religious works of art – panels, goldwork and liturgical instruments – from various churches within the diocese. *Open only 10 am–12 midday Thu–Sat; Piazzetta (behind the Duomo)*

Museo Statale di Arte Medievale e Moderna
This museum of medieval and modern art, one of the most important in the region, is housed in the Palazzo Bruni Ciocchi from the 15th century. Paintings by members of the Florentine and Aretine Schools from the 13th to the 17th centuries, a rich collection of majolica pieces and

over 3,600 coins, seals and medallions are on display here. *Open 9 am–7 pm daily; Via S. Lorentino, 8*

RESTAURANTS

Buca di S. Francesco
In the vaulted rooms of a Palazzo (14th century) next to the church, it offers excellent cuisine. *Closed Mon evening and Tue; Via S. Francesco, 1; Tel. 057 52 32 71; Category 2*

La Lancia d'Oro
This stylish restaurant is set under the Loggia del Vasari. *Closed Monday; Piazza Grande; Open 6 pm–7 pm; Tel. 057 52 10 33, Category 2*

Trattoria Il Saraceno
Only a few steps from the lively Corso Italia, a cosy *trattoria* with typical Tuscan meals at reasonable prices. *Closed Wed; Via Mazzini, 6/A; Tel. 057 52 76 44; Category 3*

Le Tastevin
Elegant restaurant with largely regional cuisine. *Closed Sun; Via de'Cenci, 9; Tel. 057 52 83 04; Category 2*

SHOPPING

In Arezzo and environs you can buy gold and silverware, ceramics, straw goods, forged iron and copperware. The colourful *weekly market* on the ✪*Piazza S. Agostino* is great for grocery shopping on Saturday mornings. The *Fiera Antiquaria*, an antiques market with over 800 stands, takes place on the first weekend of each month on the *Piazza Grande* and in the sur-

The medieval Piazza Grande in Arezzo: focal point and market square

rounding streets. It is one of the most well-known in Italy. Two tips for bargain-hunters just outside the city: in *Castiglion Fibocchi* (10 km in the direction of Reggello) there is *Gina Lebole*: tailored suits, coats, and shoes – all Lebole products are made here and sold at a discount of 35 per cent. *(Open 3.30 pm–7.30 pm Mon–Fri; Via G. Fracassi, no credit cards).* The *spaccio* occupied by *Gucci* is both expensive and elegant and includes a café – the short drive is worth it, as all articles purchased directly from the factory are considerably cheaper *(Open 9 am–6 pm Mon and Wed–Fri, 9 am–1 pm Tue; Via Aretina 63; 55 km to the north in Leccio di Reggello on the SS 69).*

ACCOMMODATION

Hotel Continentale

Centrally located on the busy Guido Monaco square near the station. Good restaurant. Facilities for the disabled. *74 rooms; Piazza Guido Monaco, 7; Tel. 057 52 02 51; Fax 05 75 35 04 85; Category 2*

Casa della Gioventù S. Severi (youth hostel)

Nice and new with 68 beds. Facilities for the disabled. *Closed Oct–Easter; Via F. Redi, 13; Tel. and Fax 05 75 29 90 47*

Hotel Minerva

Modern, pleasant building with a restaurant. Near the motorway exit, where there is a bus into the town centre. Facilities for the disabled. *118 rooms; Via Fiorentina, 4; Tel. 05 75 37 03 90; Fax 05 75 30 24 15; Category 2*

ENTERTAINMENT

Go dancing at the *Roxy Rose Disco Club (Viale Michelangelo, 48).* In the winter months there are performances in the cute *Teatro Petrarca (Via Guido Monaco, 12).*

INFORMATION

Piazza Risorgimento, 116, 52100 Arezzo; Tel. 05 75 37 76 78; Fax 057 52 08 39

SURROUNDING AREA

Anghiari   (111/D1-2)

A perfectly straight road links the elevated town of Anghiari (pop. 6,000) with Sansepolcro in the valley. Parts of the town, which still exhibits a strong medieval character, were built outside the town walls along the steep road. Well worth a look are an octagonal *abbey church* from around 1000 A.D., the church of *S. Agostino* (13th–15th centuries), and the *Palazzo Comunale*, all containing priceless works of art. *S. Stefano* church, at the foot of the hill, dates back to the 6th century and is one of the oldest churches in this area.

In the *Palazzo Taglieschi* one finds the *Museo dell'Alta Valle del Tevere* with folkloric pieces *(Open daily 9 am–7 pm).* In 1440 a battle was fought on the Anghiari plain between Florentine and Milanese forces. Leonardo da Vinci attempted to depict this in a colossal painting in the Palazzo Vecchio in Florence. You can dine and stay overnight in comfort at a manor 4 km south, the *Castello di Sorci (Closed Monday; Tel. 05 75 78 90 66; Fax 05 75 78 80 22; Category 3).*

Caprese Michelangelo (111/D1)
This village of just 1,800 inhabitants is situated on the peak of a mountain and is most renowned as the birthplace of Michelangelo Buonarroti on 6 March 1475. The house, in which his father acted as the *podestà* (mayor), today houses the *Museo Michelangiolesco* and contains documents from the artist's life *(9.30 am–6.30 pm Mon–Fri, 9.30 am–7.30 pm Sat and Sun)*. The restored section of the nearby *castle* houses plaster copies of Michelangelo's works.

Casentino (106/C6,107/D6,111/D1)
The region known as Casentino is situated along the upper reaches of the Arno and extends roughly from Stia, east of Florence, to the far side of Arezzo. The area is rarely visited by tourists despite the beauty of its wooded peaks, gently sloping valleys and precipitous Apennine passes. Casetino is also very interesting for historical reasons. Dante Alighieri often mentions the region in his works, as he personally took part in the bloody battle which raged on the Campaldino Plain near Poppi. This engagement in 1289 ended centuries of fighting between the Guelfs and Ghibellines. The landscape is dominated by many *medieval stone castles,* such as those in *Romena, Porciano, Urbech, Castelnuovo, Chitignano, Castellone* and *Poppi.* The beautiful Romanesque *baptismal churches* (Pieve) in *Gropina, Romena, Montemignaio, Socano* (which also has the largest known Etruscan temple) and *Setina* all provide an insight into the religious life of the people at the time, as do the notable *monasteries* in *Vallombrosa (Open 3 pm Sun, and in summer also 10.30 am Tue and Fri), Camaldoli* and *La Verna.*

To explore the area, take the SS 67 at Pontassieve and continue along this road through Rufina. About 10 km down this road, turn right onto the 556 toward Londa. The road – with wonderful views – climbs steeply to reach an altitude of almost 1,000 metres. The Arno has its origin at this point, to the west of the church S. Maria delle Grazie. The road drops down toward Stia (where you can make a 4 km-detour to the *Castel di Romena* and the lovely *Pieve*). It then continues on toward *Pratovecchio* – reputably the birthplace of the painter Paolo Uccello (1397–1475) – and to *Poppi* which has a *castle* belonging to Count Guidi. Arnolfo di Cambio reputedly took this fortress as a model for the Palazzo Vecchio in Florence *(Castello open daily 9.30 am–12.30 pm and 3 pm–6 pm)*. Here the road heads toward *Camaldoli Hermitage* (1,104 m), where you can view the stone cells of hermits, located behind a wall in the forest *(Monastery hospice Tel. 05 75 55 60 13; closed Jan–March)*. After driving to *Bibbiena,* the main town of the Casentino region with its ancient town centre, you take the picturesque route (208) in an easterly direction to reach the *Franciscan shrine* on Monte La Verna (1,128 m). It was here that St. Francis of Assisi received his stigma in 1224. The monastery complex, containing works of art and the grotto in which the saint lived, is open to the public *(Open daily 8 am–8 pm)*. There is also a hospice with restaurant *(Pastor Angelicus; closed Oct–Easter; Chiusi della Verna; Tel. 05 75 59 90 25; Category 3)*. In this heavily-wooded area boasting abundant game, there are some very good restaurants and delightful hotels, such as the *Ristorante Il Cedro* which offers good, simple food in the town of *Moggiona* near Camaldoli *(Closed Monday; Tel. 05 75 55 60 80; Category 2–3)* and *Hotel Ristorante Villa Rigacci*, which serves excellent meals in a stylish villa situated in a large park in *Reggello-Vaggio(23 rooms; Tel. 05 58 65 65 62; Fax 05 58 65 65 37; Category 1–2)*.

Cortona (111/D3)

٭ Built on a mountain at an altitude of 495 metres, this medieval city (pop. 23,000) with its steep, narrow laneways and steps overlooks the valley. Cortona was also one of the 12 Etruscan *Lukomonie* and remnants of the imposing town walls are still visible. The *Palazzo Casali* (13th/15th centuries) contains substantial relics and artefacts from Etruscan tombs, such as a unique bronze chandelier and valuable paintings, which include some by Pinturicchio, Luca Signorelli and Gino Severini, the latter two born in Cortona *(Museo dell'Accademia Etrusca; Open 10 am–1 pm and 4–7 pm Tue–Sun; Piazza Signorelli)*.

On the centrally located *Piazza della Repubblica* one finds the *Palazzo Comunale* (13th century), with its tower and beautiful external stairway, and the *Loggia del Grano* (grain store). From here you can enter the lovely *Teatro Signorelli* (1857). Next to the *Duomo* (16th century) is the *Museo Diocesano d'Arte Sacra (Open 9.30 am–1 pm and 3.30 pm–7 pm Tue–Sun)*; especially impressive are the *Annunciation* by Beato Angelico and two painted crucifixes

by Pietro Lorenzetti. From the ٭ terrace of the *Piazza Garibaldi* one has a marvellous view of the plain, with Lake Trasimeno and Monte Amiata in the distance. Excursions to the nearby *Celle monastery* (4 km), founded by Francis of Assisi in 1211, or to the *Castello di Montecchio Vesponi* (13th century) seven kilometres away, are well worthwhile. In the town itself you can buy inexpensive ceramics, antiques and wine. A good place to stay is the *Hotel San Luca* , which includes the *Ristorante Tonino (Closed Mon evening and Tue; 57 rooms; Tel. 05 75 63 04 60; Fax 75 63 01 05; Both Category 2)*.

Lucignano (110/C3)

Circular fortress-like village with its medieval townscape still intact. In the *Palazzo Comunale* there are impressive frescos by artists belonging to the Aretine and Sienese Schools *(Open 10 am–1 pm and 4 pm–7 pm Tue–Sun)*.

Monterchi (111/E2)

In Etruscan-Roman times the square of the small village was a place dedicated to the worship of the deity Hercules. Today one drives to Monterchi primarily to admire the fresco *Madonna del Parto* (about 1445) by Piero della Francesca, which has been removed from the wall of the cemetery chapel *(Open 9 am–1 pm and 2 pm–7 pm Tue–Sun, in summer also 9.30 pm–12 midnight; Scuola Elementare, Via Reglia)*.

Monte San Savino (110/C3)

We can probably thank Andrea Contucci, known as Sansovino, for the fact that Renaissance architecture is the dominant style here. Born here in about 1460, he built the *S. Agostino* monastery. The *Loggia dei Mercanti* (market hall) is also attributed to him. The imposing *Palazzo Ciocchi del Monte* (1516), which today houses the town hall, is the work of Antonio da Sangallo the Elder. Other buildings open to the public are the *Museo della Ceramica (Open daily 9.30 am–12.30 pm and 4–7 pm)* with its fascinating collection and the ◁▷ *Torre Civica* watch-tower *(Open 9.30 am–12.30 pm and 4 pm–7 pm Sat and Sun),* where there is a breathtaking view of the countryside. In nearby *Castello di Gargonza*, a village entirely surrounded by the 13th-century castle walls, 19 farmhouses have been lovingly restored as holiday apartments. Just outside the walls is a very good restaurant *(Azienda Castello di Gargonza; Tel. 05 75 84 70 21; Fax 05 75 84 70 54; Category 2).*

Sansepolcro (111/E1)

Piero della Francesca was born here and he died here. Sansepolcro lies on the broad Tiberian plain, the medieval section of the town still surrounded by a quadrangular wall. In the *Museo Civico* you will find two important works by Piero: the large winged altar *Madonna della Misericordia* and the *Resurrezione (Open daily 9.30 am–1.30 pm and 2.30 pm–7.30 pm).* Also worth a look are the Romanesque *cathedral* and *S. Francesco* church. In the suburb of Pieve Vecchia you can find very attractive lodgings and excellent cuisine (reservations necessary) at *Albergo Ristorante dell'Oroscopo di Paola e Marco Mercati (Closed midday and Sun; 12 rooms; Via Palmiro Togliatti, 68; Tel. and Fax 05 75 73 48 75; Hotel Category 3; Restaurant Category 2).* The city (pop.

17,000) is also famous for the furniture and lace produced here.

Sinalunga (110/C3)

◁▷ This delightful medieval town (pop. 12,000) with a lovely Baroque church lies 30 km to the southwest. Two km further south is the *Locanda dell'Amorosa*, an exceptionally well-preserved estate complex with an excellent restaurant and 15 rooms *(Closed Tue midday and Mon; Tel. 05 77 67 94 97; Fax 05 7 63 20 01; Category 1).*

Valdichiana (111/D2–4)

Broad and fertile, the Chiana Valley extends southward like a garden from Arezzo to Chiusi on the border to Umbria. The Chiana Valley, which the Autostrada A1 to Rome dissects, was once Etruria's bread basket. The white Chianina cattle are still bred today, their meat used to prepare *bistecca alla fiorentina.* An excellent white wine, the Bianco Vergine, is also produced here – it is best to buy it at the *Cantina Sociale di Cortona* at the foot of the mountain in *Camucia; Viale A. Gramsci, 113.*

Valtiberina (107/D5–6)

The Tiber (Tevere) has its source on Monte Fumaiolo in the Apennine range at an altitude of 1,407 m, a few kilometres from the source of the Arno. In the vicinity of Arezzo both rivers run parallel to each other – only separated by the Alpe di Catenaia range. The Tiber Valley is harsher and more precipitous than that of the Arno – for this reason grazing and forestry are still the main sources of income in the area. All of Valtiberina is cut by the Superstrada (highway) 3, which links Rome and Ravenna.

Marble and Maremma

From the Leaning Tower of Pisa to invigorating seaside activities

Variety is most certainly guaranteed along Tuscany's 300-km coastal strip. There are world-famous, picturesque cities, extensive national parks and ancient Etruscan tombs – and plenty of aquatic fun.

ELBA

(108/C6) ★ The island of Elba (pop. 29,000) is a mini-paradise – especially in spring and at the beginning of autumn, when the flood of tourists has subsided somewhat. Elba's natural features are quite varied, alternating between scrub-like woods, pine forests, vineyards, orchards and steep rocky cliffs with sandy, crescent-shaped beaches. The highest point on the island is the 1,019-m *Monte Capanne (accessible by gondola from Marciana Alta)*, which has medieval villages hugging its steep, rocky slopes. The island has been inhabited since before

Even if you can no longer climb up it, the biggest attraction in Pisa remains the world-famous Leaning Tower

Christ, and in the years 1814–15 Napoleon spent nine months and 21 days here in exile – and left objects which now constitute one of the biggest tourist attractions on the island. In 1996 Elba and the surrounding marine waters were declared a national park, the *Parco Nazionale dell'Arcipelago Toscano*. Those interested in Geology should pop in to the *Mineralogical Museum* in *Rio Marina* . Napoleon fans can visit the *Palazzina dei Mulini* in *Portoferraio* and *Villa San Martino* along the road to Procchio.

RESTAURANTS

Publius
*Publius is particularly well-known for its outstanding game dishes. There are also spectacular views from along the northern coastal road. *Closed Mon and Nov–Mar; Poggio, Piazza XX Settembre; Tel. 056 59 92 08; Category 2*

Rendezvous da Marcello
Located directly on the harbour, it offers the perfect *ambiente* to enjoy seafood. *Closed Wed; Marci-*

ana Marina, Piazza della Vittoria, 1;
Tel. 056 59 92 51; Category 2

ACCOMMODATION

Piccolo Hotel Barsalini
Situated on the small S. Andrea Bay,
with its coarse sandy beach, is a
quaint hotel serving excellent cuisine. *30 rooms; Closed Nov–Mar; Marciana Capo S. Andrea; Tel 05 65 90 80
13; Fax 05 65 90 82 64; Category 2–3*

Pensione Casa Rosa
A family-run establishment with
excellent meals, it is just 150 m
from the beach and also has its
own tennis courts. *35 rooms;
Closed Nov–April; Portoferraio,
Località La Biodola; Tel. and Fax
0565 96 99 31 and 05 65 96 98 57;
Category 3*

Hotel Fabricia
Spacious, modern hotel with a children's playground, tennis courts,
garden, pool, sandy beach. *76 rooms;
Closed Nov–March; Portoferraio, Località Magazzini; Tel. 05 65 93 31 81;
Fax 05 65 93 31 85; Category 1*

Hotel Hermitage
The oldest luxury hotel on the island, with additional bungalows set
in the pine forest. It has its own golf
course and half-board is manda-
tory. *138 rooms; Closed Nov–April,
Portoferraio, Località La Biodola; Tel.
05 65 93 69 11; Fax 05 65 96 99 84;
Category 1*

GETTING THERE

The most popular place to get a
ferry to Elba is Piombino harbour.

MARCO POLO SELECTION:
COASTAL AREAS

1 Carrara
The 'marble city' set be-
tween the quarries of the
Apuan Alps and the ele-
gant seaside resorts of
the Versilia (page 69)

2 Campo dei Miracoli in Pisa
The Leaning Tower, Duomo
and Baptistery form a
monumental religious and
architectural ensemble
(pages 72 and 73)

**3 Parco Naturale
della Maremma**
The most diverse natural
reserve in Tuscany stretches
for 20 km along the coast
(page 61)

**4 Populonia
on the Gulf of Baratti**
Combine a visit to the Etruscan tombs with a swim in the
picturesque gulf (page 66)

5 Arcipelago Toscano
The waters around the islands
of Elba and Giglio offer the
best diving, while the entire
region is a mecca for sailors
and windsurfers alike
(pages 57 and 59)

6 Sovana
This medieval town lies above
the most extensive Etruscan
necropolis, with tombs from
the 2nd and 3rd centuries
B.C. (page 63)

Most boats from the mainland dock in Portoferraio harbour

In summer the ferries leave approximately every hour from 6.10 am–8.50 pm. Prices vary seasonally between L10,000–15,000 per person (the trip to Portoferraio takes 60 minutes).

GIGLIO

(112/A5) ★ This small, steep, forested, rocky island with 28 km of coastline has a number of tiny sandy bays with crystal clear water, making it ideal for scuba diving. There is a ferry service several times a day from Porto S. Stefano (1-hour trip). The boats dock in the quaint, picturesque harbour of Giglio Porto. To the west of the seaside town of Giglio Campese there is a fully preserved fortress, Giglio Castello, situated on the island's highest peak. Two highly-recommendable hotels are the ☼ *Castello Monticello* overlooking the harbour, with a magnificent view and parking *(34 rooms; Closed Oct–Easter time; Tel. 05 64 80 92 52; Fax 05 64 80 94 73; Category 2)* and the classically Mediterranean *Hotel Campese*,

located directly on the island's most gorgeous beach *(39 rooms; Closed Oct–Easter; Tel. 05 64 80 40 03; Fax 05 64 80 40 93; Category 2)*. It's best to leave your car on the mainland and just use the local bus services.

GROSSETO

(112/B2-3) Situated on the plain at the mouth of the Ombrone River, Grosseto (pop. 71,000) has developed into one of southern Tuscany's major agricultural centres over the course of the 20th century. This feat has only been achieved after hundreds of years of draining the swamps which covered great expanses of this malaria-infested region. It is also still possible to walk along the bastions of the star-shaped defensive wall surrounding the city, which was built before Grosseto fell under Florentine and Medici rule in the 16th century.

SIGHTS

The historic centre is certainly worth strolling through,

with highlights being the *Duomo* and the church of *S. Francesco*, which features an exceptionally beautiful crucifix by Duccio da Buoninsegna.

MUSEUMS

Museo Archeologico e d'Arte della Maremma and Museo Diocesano d'Arte Sacra

Both museums are housed in the one palace. The archaeological museum exhibits artefacts found throughout the province, mostly of Etruscan heritage. The Museo Diocesano has majolica pieces and small artworks by the Sienese School. *Currently closed due to reorganization; Piazza Baccarini, 3; Tel. 05 64 45 51 32*

RESTAURANTS

Ristorante Buca San Lorenzo

Located directly in the shadows of the town's defensive wall, it is quite elegant and the chef is very creative. *Closed Sun; Viale Manetti, 1; Tel. 056 42 51 42; Category 2*

Osteria del Ponte Rotto

10 km from Grosseto on the road to Scansano. Fine, hearty traditional cuisine, served under a shady pergola overlooking the river in summer. *Closed Wed; Istia d'Ombrone; Via Scansano, 636; Tel. 05 64 40 93 73; Category 3*

SHOPPING

The Maremma is renowned for its *pecorino* (sheep's milk cheese) and its wild boar products. Both can be purchased at the *weekly market* held every Thursday morning on the *Piazza del Mercato* in Grosseto. At the *Bottega del Seggiolaio (Via Chiasso*

degli Zuavi, 5A) the *butteri,* the Maremma cowboys, still make the famous rocking chairs as well as the traditional Tuscan wicker stools and armchairs.

ACCOMMODATION

Grand Hotel Bastiani

In the city centre, but without its own restaurant. *48 rooms; Piazza Gioberti, 64; Tel. 056 42 00 47; Fax 056 42 93 21; Category 1–2*

Albergo Maremma

Also in the centre of town, it has a cosy restaurant *(Tel. 056 42 11 77; Closed Sun evening and Mon). 34 rooms; Via F. Paolucci de'Calboli, 11; Tel. 056 42 22 93; Fax 056 42 20 51; Category 2*

Mediterraneo

13 km to the west in Marina di Grosseto, situated directly on the coast. *52 rooms; Viale 24 Maggio, 70; Tel. 056 43 45 00; Fax 056 43 52 61; Category 2*

INFORMATION

Via Monterosa, 206, 58100 Grosseto, Tel. 05 64 45 45 27, Fax 05 64 45 46 06

SURROUNDING AREA

Ansedonia   (112/C5)

The *Tagliata Etrusca*, a canal cut right into the rock, regulates the ocean flowing in and out and prevents the harbour from silting up. The *museum (Open daily 9 am–2 pm Oct–Mar; 9 am–7 pm April–Sept)* is situated directly within the Scavi di Cosa excavation site. Both these attractions make a visit to this old Etruscan town by the sea well worthwhile.

Capalbio   (112/C4)

A mountain village situated in the most southern area of the Maremma region. Each year a game festival is held here. Drop into the *sculpture museum* run by the sculptor Niki de Saint-Phalle *(Open 2.30 pm–7.30 pm Mon–Fri, mid-March–Oct; take the Pescia Fiorentina exit on the SS1, and then drive 1 km inland).* Also avail yourself of the opportunity to savour some of the local game specialities at the *trattorie Da Maria (Closed Tue; Tel. 05 64 89 60 14; Category 2)* and *La Porta (Closed Tue; Tel. 05 64 89 63 11; Category 2–3).*

Colline Metallifere   (109/E–F3–4)

Extending from Saline di Volterra to Massa Marittima (with geothermal spa baths at Larderello on the way), the picturesque SS439 dissects the northern Maremma region. Centuries ago, Etruscans and Romans mined ore in these metal-bearing hills for the production of silver, iron and copper. Today almost all the mines here are closed.

Lago di Burano   (112/C5)

✪ ⚑ These 300 hectares of swamp feeding into the sea constitute one of the last remaining havens for many water birds. Access is from the Aurelia exit on the SS1 near Capalbio Stazione. *Tours 10 am and 2 pm Sun, Sept–April; Closed May–Aug for the nesting season.*

Massa Marittima   (112/A1)

〰 The 'Jewel of the Maremma' (pop. 10,000) is perched 380 m above dark forests. Its Romanesque-Gothic *Duomo S. Cerbone* is one of the most splendid in Tuscany. The cathedral square is bordered by the *Palazzo Pretorio (Museo Archeologico),* the *Palazzo Comunale* (with the famous *Maestà* by Ambrogio Lorenzetti) and *Count Biserno's Palazzo* from the 13th century. Of great interest are the *Museo della Miniera (housed in an old mine shaft, but currently closed for renovations)* and the *Centro Carapax on the plain (Open 9.30 am–12.30 pm and 2.30 pm–5.30 pm Sat and Sun, Oct–May; Open daily 9.30 am–12.30 pm and 4 pm–7 pm, June–Sept; Closed 24 Dec–3 Jan).* The Centro is home to hundreds of tortoises and white storks which can be observed in the wild. Accommodation is available at the *Hotel Il Sole (50 rooms; Via della Libertà, 43; Tel. 05 66 90 19 71; Fax 05 66 90 19 59; Category 3).*

Monte Argentario   (112/B4–5)

〰 Blossoming gardens and hidden villas, crystal clear water and small sandy inlets make this peninsula the perfect home away from home for the rich and famous on holiday. The major town is *Porto S. Stefano,* located in the north (with a ferry to Giglio and a yacht harbour), while the exclusive *Port'Ercole* lies in the south.

Parco Naturale della Maremma   (112/B3–4)

★ An infamous swamp until the 1930s, the fertile coastal plain of the Maremma with its dense scrub-cloaked hills as a backdrop has become a popular destination for independent holiday-makers. The western part of this region is now a national park *(Parco Naturale dell' Uccellina)* with more species of wildlife than any other in Tuscany (water birds, buffalo, wild horses). It extends along the coast for 20 km from Principina al Mare in the north to Talamone in the south and is 4 km wide at some points. You can get a bus from *Alberese,* where you can also obtain tickets for the park. There are walks of various length, but dogs are not allowed. *Open 7 am–4 pm Wed, Sat, and Sun, 16 June–30 Sept; Otherwise free entrance from 9 am to 1 hour before sunset.*

Pitigliano (113/D3)

〰️ Pitigliano (pop. 4,000) is perched spectacularly on a plateau, high above cliffs carved out by the Lente River. The medieval buildings, vineyards and aquaduct appear to grow out of the tuff (soft limestone) cliffs, which are riddled with the caves used to mature the famous local Bianco di Pitigliano wine. The *Cantina Cooperativa Narrisi e Bussi (Via S. Chiara, 17)* is a good place to acquire some. You can try some in the restaurant of the hotel *Albergo Guastini (27 rooms, Piazza Petruccioli; Tel. 05 64 61 60 65; Fax 05 64 61 66 52; Category 3).* Twenty km to the east, on the panoramic SS74, you come to the *Lago di Bolsena,* located in the neighbouring province of Lazio.

Punta Ala (109/E6)

A totally artificial holiday village, but done well. This peninsula is directly across the water from Elba. With 900 berths, it has the largest yacht harbour on the Tyrrhenian coast, as well as the most spectacular golf course, bridle paths, a polo field, apartment buildings and four top-class hotels, with all the comforts you could ever need and facilities for the disabled.

Roselle (112/B2)

The most significant Etruscan-Roman *excavation site* in the area (Cyclopean wall, amphitheatre, forum and villa) lies 350 m above the Salica River on an old Roman road, surrounded by forest. *Open daily from 9 am–5.30 pm Nov–Feb; 9 am–6.30 pm Mar–Apr; 9 am–7.30 pm May–Aug; 9 am to sunset Sept–Oct; Take the SS 223 from Grosseto towards Siena for 10 km*

Saturnia (112/C3)

Sulphurous 37°C (98°F) water springs at a rate of 800 litres per second from this volcanic crater,

Nothing beats a splash in the hot sulphurous springs in Saturnia

which has unfortunately been converted into a swimming pool. The ✪ *Terme di Saturnia Hotel* utilizes this natural resource for their health spas. To the south, one can take an invigorating bath free of charge in the tuff pools set amidst natural ⚲ *waterfalls.* Half an hour away there are the Etruscan sites belonging to the *Pian di Palma* – despite the difficulties getting there the effort is well worth it! Accommodation can be found at the *Hotel Terme di Saturnia,* which in 1988 received the Italian hotel industry's equivalent to an Oscar *(92 rooms; Tel. 05 64 60 10 61; Fax 05 64 60 12 66; Category 1).* A great restaurant and twelve reasonably-priced rooms are to be found at the *Locanda Laudomia (closed Wed; Tel. 05 64 62 00 62; Fax 05 64 62 00 13; Category 3).*

Sovana (113/D3)

★ A quaint Etruscan village situated on a tuff plateau above dense forest with a beautiful Romanesque *Duomo.* The *Palazzetto Pretorio* houses the *Centro Documentale del Territorio Sovanese* which contains extensive documentation on the nearby necropolis. A local guide for visiting the tombs can be hired in the *Taverna Etrusca,* where you are provided with food and beverages free of charge. They also have eight rooms for overnight guests *(Closed Mon; Tel. 05 64 61 61 83; Fax 05 64 61 41 93; Category 2–3).*

Talamone (112/B4)

⚲ A tiny fishing village at the foot of a rocky spur overlooking a pretty bay (swimming possible) with harbour facilities. There are some fine fish restaurants. The *Albergo Capo d'Uomo,* high above the ocean, offers

accommodation with facilities for the disabled *(Closed Oct–April; 24 rooms; Tel. 05 64 88 70 77; Fax 05 64 88 72 98; Category 2).*

Vetulonia (112/A2)

⬥ 346 m above sea level and set in olive groves, this village is built on top of the ruins of an important Etruscan centre. The view over the Maremma is magnificent. A noteworthy *necropolis* is located on the plain.

Vulci (113/D5)

What was once one of the wealthiest and largest Etruscan cities on the Fiora River plain is today an overgrown field which has been subject over the years to extensive plundering by grave robbers. The *François tomb* is really quite remarkable.

LIVORNO

(108/1–2) Livorno (pop. 168,000) is the second largest city in Tuscany and has the largest harbour, which dominates life here with its kilometres of container and refinery facilities. The oldest part of the city is criss-crossed by canals, and the bastions surrounding the former harbour (Porto Mediceo) testify to the city's previous significance.

Although Livorno was a naval outpost back in Roman times, it always remained in Pisa's shadow until the 16th century, when the grand dukes of Florence built it up to be their major harbour. In 1576 they even commissioned the master builder Bernardo Buontalenti to create an 'ideal pentagonal city'. Today, little can be seen of this work as Livorno was severely damaged during World War II. In 1593 the Costituzione Livor-

Harbour and castle in Livorno

and other 'Macchiaioli' (a group of artists closely linked to the Impressionists), but also prehistoric relics. The villa is surrounded by a shady park. *Open 10 am–1 pm and 4 pm–7 pm Tue–Sun; Villa Mimbelli; Via S. Jacopo in Acquaviva*

nina was enacted, which guaranteed freedom and protection to all persons seeking asylum. This display of tolerance brought people of various races and religions to settle here. For example, Livorno had one of the most substantial and wealthiest Jewish communities in all Italy. Livorno's most famous sons are the painters Amedeo Modigliani and Giovanni Fattori and the composer Pietro Mascagni.

SIGHTS

Acquario Comunale
✪ ⚡ A huge range of Mediterranean fauna presented in glass cabinets. *Open 9.30 am–12.30 pm and 4 pm–7 pm Tue–Sun (Winter 2.30 pm–5.30 pm); Piazzale Mascagni*

Boat tours
In the summer months the harbour authorities conduct boat tours through the canals of the old city district of 'Mini Venice'. *Information: Tel. 05 86 84 17 34*

MUSEUM

Museo Civico Giovanni Fattori
The museum holds not only many works by Giovanni Fattoris

RESTAURANTS

Livornese fish dishes are famous, especially the fish soup known as *cacciucco*.

Antico Moro
✪ A classic establishment in an alley near the market – great fish dishes. *Closed Tue–Sat midday and Wed; Via E. Bartelloni, 59; Tel. 05 86 88 46 59; Category 2*

La Barcarola
According to the Livornese, Beppino makes the best *cacciucco*, as well as other delicious dishes. Near the station. *Closed Sun; Viale Carducci, 63; Tel. 05 86 40 23 67; Category 2*

Siciliani
✪ Located directly on Porto Mediceo. Wharf labourers and genuine cuisine. *Piazzale del Marcus (Toremar Ferries wharf); No Tel.; Category 3*

La Vecchia Senese
Tuscan, Neapolitan – and fish. *Closed Sun; Via del Tempio, 14; Tel. 05 86 89 25 60; Category 2–3*

SHOPPING

The smartest shops are located along the ✪ *Via Grande*.

Mercatino Americano
✪ ⚡ From parachutes to cold cream, you can find almost anything at the large market held at

his former American army base. *Open 9 am–7.30 pm Tue–Sat; Piazza XX Settembre*

Mercato Nuovo
❖ This market, situated in a wrought-iron structure typical of the turn of the century and also on the square before it, offers a complete range of Mediterranean-style cooking ingredients. *Open 9 am–1 pm Tue–Sat; Via del Cardinale*

ACCOMMODATION

Gran Duca
Located directly on Porto Mediceo, with an outstanding restaurant *(Closed Mon midday)*. *62 rooms; Piazza Micheli, 16; Tel. 05 86 89 10 24; Fax 05 86 89 11 53; Category 2*

Romito
↘ 10 km to the south on the SS1, situated on a steep coastal stretch. Large terrace and all 15 rooms overlook the ocean directly. A fine restaurant *(Closed Wed). Via Aurelia, 274; Tel. and Fax 05 86 58 05 20; Category 2–3*

SPORTS & LEISURE

In the suburb of Ardenza there is a famous horse racing track ❖ *F. Caprilli.*

INFORMATION

Piazza Cavour, 6, 57126 Livorno; Tel. 05 86 89 81 1; Fax 05 86 89 61 73

SURROUNDING AREA

Bolgheri (109/D3)
The most beautiful, longest (4.8 km) and most famous cypress avenue in all Italy leads to Gherardesca Castle, from where you can enter the medieval hamlet. To the right and left are olive groves and vineyards. The renowned Sassicaia wine, the most famous (and most expensive) wine currently available in Italy, is produced from these grapes. Whoever happens to be in the area around Easter time should take a look at the nocturnal ❖ *Good Friday procession*, lit by flaming torches. Cosy *trattorie* tempt one to indulge in the culinary specialities of the area, especially the wild boar ham and the sausages! Try some of their outstanding wine – it doesn't necessarily have to be a Sassicaia.

Castiglioncello (109/D2)
❖ With its crescent-shaped sandy beaches and narrow, rocky inlets (swimming possible), it is a coastal gem, frequented almost exclusively by Italians and offering the best swimming and night life along this coast. At the southern end, in *Caletta,* you will find **La Marinella**, a quaint *pensione* at the water's edge and open the whole year round *(21 rooms; Via Giovanni Marradi, 12; Tel. 05 86 79 42 04; Fax 05 86 75 40 82; Category 3)*. More elegant, with a tennis court and swimming pool, is the *Villa Parisi,* overlooking the ocean from its elevated position near the Piazza *(20 rooms; Via Monti, 10; Tel. 05 86 75 16 98; Fax 05 86 75 11 67; Category 1).*

Donoratico (109/D4)
♯ Long, broad and gently sloping sandy beaches and dense pine forests are the hallmark of this seaside town, which is also particularly suitable for children.

Etruscan Riviera   (108/C2, 109/D3–5)

The coast to the south of Livorno got its name from the many Etruscan artefacts discovered in its hinterland. The 20-km stretch of sheer coastline begins directly to the south of the city, with pine forests and thick bushy woods covering the inland slopes. The ◁▷ Via Aurelia (SS1) takes you directly along the coast and in good weather you can see all the way to Corsica. A little further on, the hills move back from the coast and the beach becomes gentler. A broad, fertile plain now stretches from the ocean to Piombino, i.e. the former Maremma swamp.

Piombino   (109/D5)

A harbour city (pop. 37,000) with facilities for treating the iron ore from the neighbouring island of Elba and the nearby Colline Metallifere area. It is the major port for ferries to the Isola d'Elba. Should you get hungry before the crossing, we can recommend the *Osteria Carugi (Closed Sun; Via Ferrer, 10; Tel. 05 65 22 44 22; Category 3)*.

Populonia   (109/D5)

★ ⚓ The Baratti Gulf, with a beautiful sandy beach at the foot of the old Etruscan town, was the site of Etruria's only harbour. The ore mined on Elba and in the metalliforous mountains was melted here, and in 1908 a large necropolis was discovered in the slag heaps. The tombs are located between oleanders and pines right on the coastal road and are open to the public. The ◁▷ *Trattoria La Pergola* serves outstanding fish dishes and offers magnificent views over the ocean *(Closed on Tue in winter; Tel. 056 52 95 96; Category 2)*. If you continue further along the road up to the village of ◁▷ *Populonia* with its medieval buildings, there is an exquisite view over the gulf and the rocky coastline, all the way to Elba.

San Vincenzo   (109/D4)

✥ ⚓ A lively village (pop. 7,000) the whole year round. The Colline Metallifere hills extend right to this coastal settlement, and to the south the white sandy beaches merge with the thick pine forests which line the road all the way to the Baratti Gulf. The village has a swimming centre, free beaches and a sailing regatta which is held on 30 July and 15 August, starting from the yacht harbour. There are seafood restaurants and pizzerie for all budgets on the waterfront, but also one of the best restaurants in all Italy (make reservations), the *Ristorante Gambero Rosso*. It not only serves outstanding meals, but also sells olive oil and other delicacies *(Closed Tue; Piazza della Vittoria; Tel. 05 65 70 10 21; Category 1).*

MASSA

(104/C3–4) The province of Massa-Carrara is situated in the north-western corner of Tuscany and encompasses the Lunigiana area on both sides of the Magra Valley right up to the Cisa Pass. It is geologically and economically quite different from the rest of the province of Tuscany. Eighty per cent of the unindustrialized north is constituted by mountainous forests, with marble as practically the only source of income until 1945.

In the second half of the 19th century, poverty and hunger, combined with the arduous and dangerous work in the quarries run by the 'marble barons', had already led the marble workers to stage several unsuccessful uprisings. However, in 1902 they finally managed to push through the best labour contracts available in Italy at the time. In 1945 the FAI (Federazione Anarchica Italiana), the Italian Anarchist Federation, was founded in Carrara. Today there is still the anarchist café and an anarchist newspaper. Even the cathedral square had a panel bearing the liberal slogan 'A free square for free people', which can still be seen there.

Both Massa and Carrara are located in absolutely stunning settings, flanked by the Ligurian Sea to the west and the mountains of the Apuan Alps in the east, with their white shining marble quarries and the peaks of Monte Pisanino (1,945 m) and Monte Sagro (1,749 m). The slopes are cloaked in pine trees, olive groves, vineyards and chestnut forests up to an altitude of 700 metres. Oak and beech trees grow along the limestone slopes up to the tree line. Well-marked trails and numerous refuges *(rifugi)* make the area a paradise for nature lovers, hikers and mountain climbers alike. The Parco Nazionale delle Alpi Apuane (Apuan Alps National Park) occupies 500 square kilometres and includes practically the entire mountain range.

This area has always been popular with foreign visitors, but no other province has managed to develop so many attractions to keep holiday-makers busy. Along the coast you can laze about under the brightly coloured sun umbrellas which line the sandy white beaches or take advantage of the many sporting facilities. Simple *trattorie* serve modest cuisine and elegant restaurants more refined creations. At various *enoteche* you can enjoy snacks and sample Candia, the dry white wine from the grapes produced on the slopes of the Apuan Alps and which you can only find here. In the evening the entire coast from Marina di Carrara to Viareggio is a sickle-shaped chain of lights, where you can take a stroll under the palms along the beachfront boardwalk. Then you can either attend concerts or the theatre, sit in cafés or ice-cream parlours, or head off to discos and night clubs.

The provincial capital, Massa (pop. 67,000), is situated on both sides of the Autostrada della Versilia, stretching from the seaside resort of Marina to the heavily-wooded base of the Apuan Alps. Industrial plants now occupy the valley, and a 4.5-km tree-lined avenue leads to the ocean, with villas built in the outgoing 19th century. Built on a mountainside, the city has narrow winding alleys and is partially surrounded by a city wall. It also has palm trees and large quantities of white marble – not very typical for the region.

SIGHTS

Castello Malaspina
⬥⬥ The former castle above the town was converted into a Renaissance palace in the 16th century. Wonderful view of the ocean! *Only open for exhibitions*

Duomo
Beautiful marble façade, Baroque interior and a royal vault.

Palazzo Cybo-Malaspina
❖ A gloomy palace built in 1560 with an attractive inner courtyard and arcades (today it houses prefectural offices). *Piazza Aranci*

MUSEUM

Museo Etnologico delle Apuane
Over 100,000 artefacts and documents concerning life and customs in the Alpi Apuane area are on exhibition here. *Entry only after prior booking; Tel. 05 85 25 13 30; Via Uliveto, 85*

RESTAURANTS

Il Bottaccio
This old oil mill 5 km outside the town has been converted into a first-class restaurant of impeccable Italian design. Also (luxury) apartments. *Closed Mon in winter; Montignoso; Tel. 05 85 34 00 31; Fax 05 85 34 01 03, Category 1*

La Lanterna Verde
Near the beach in Marina di Massa with traditional local meals and pizza. *Closed Wed in winter; Via*

A sea of shade in Marina di Massa on the Versilia coast

delle Pinete, 71; Tel. 05 85 24 17 89; Category 3

Il Passeggero

Fine restaurant in an old vault on the Piazza Aranci. *Closed Sun; Via Alberica, 2; Tel. 05 85 48 96 51; Category 2–3*

ACCOMMODATION

The *Galleria in Massa can be recommended (18 rooms; Viale della Democrazia, 2; Tel. 058 54 21 37; Fax 05 85 48 91 06; Category 3).* In Marina di Massa you can find some hotels which are open throughout the year, and also a lovely *youth hostel* situated directly on the beach *(Open Easter–Oct; Via delle Pinete, 237; Tel. 05 85 78 00 34; Fax 05 85 78 06 59).*

ENTERTAINMENT

The seaside town of Marina di Massa offers a broad range of evening entertainment during the summer season – but from November to May there are only the performances at the *Teatro Comunale* in Massa.

INFORMATION

Lungomare Vespucci, 24, 54037 Marina di Massa; Tel. 05 85 24 00 63; Fax 05 85 86 90 15

SURROUNDING AREA

Carrara (104/B3)

★ The marble city (pop. 67,000) is located 100 m higher above sea level than its sister city 5 km away. Its name is derived from 'kar', which means stone. Here marble blocks wait to be loaded,

and the 'Milk Stream', turned white by the dust from marble cutting, flows through the city. The *Palazzo Malaspina* (16th century), with its beautiful inner courtyard, is home to the *Accademia di Belle Arti*, the Art Academy. A fine collection of marble Roman statues from Luni and the marble quarries is on view there *(Open 9 am–12 midday Mon–Fri; Via Roma, 1).* Every two years (2000/2002), from mid July until the beginning of August, the *Piazza Alberica* becomes an open-air atelier, where you can watch sculptors from around the world at work. The Romanesque-Gothic *Duomo* (11th century) is clad in marble and the *Titan Fountain* by Baccio Bandinelli is entirely of marble.

Forte dei Marmi (104/C4)

❂The finest resort on the northern coastal fringe of Tuscany and the prices reflect this. Elegant shops, neat beach, the finest restaurants *(La Barca; Closed Tue midday and Mon; Viale Italico, 3; Tel. 058 48 93 23; Category 1),* luxury hotels *(Byron; 24 rooms; Viale Morin, 46; Tel. 05 84 78 70 52; Fax 05 84 78 71 52; Category 1)* and the most fashionable night-life. 37 tennis courts and an 18-hole golf course supplement the facilities. *Information: Viale Achille Franceschi, 8 b, 55042 Forte dei Marmi; Tel. 058 48 00 91; Fax 058 48 32 14*

Lido di Camaiore (104/C4)

�433A very family-oriented seaside resort with a sandy 3-km beach and a big children's playground in the Pineta. If you feel like an informal meal, the *Ristorante Ariston Mare*, directly on the water,

Even its name testifies to the significance marble has had in this area throughout the ages: Pietrasanta – 'Holy Stone'

can be recommended *(Only open in the evening – except Sat and Sun; also open midday Oct–May, but closed Mon; Viale Colombo, 660; Tel. 05 84 90 47 47; Category 2).*

Lunigiana (104/A–B1–2)

Take the winding, scenic route along the SS62 to the Cisa Pass (1,039 m), with castles lining both sides of the road. In *Sorano* there is a lovely Romanesque *pieve* (village church). *Pontremoli* is really worth visiting, especially for its churches *S. Annunziata* (16th century), *S. Francesco* and the Baroque *Duomo*. The *Castello Piagnaro* (15th century) contains a *museum* with steles from the 1st and 2nd millennia B.C. which have been found in the area: *Museo delle Statue–Stele Lunigianesi (Open 9 am–12 midday and 3 pm–6 pm Tue–Sun; in winter open 9 am–12 midday and 2 pm–5 pm;*

closed 1 Jan, 1 May and 25 Dec). Game dishes and mushrooms head the bill in local Lunigiana cuisine, but chestnut desserts are also popular. You can find small hotels and outstanding restaurants everywhere. Of particular note is the *Trattoria del Giardino* in *Pontremoli*, where you can also buy local produce *(Closed Sun evening and Mon in winter; Via Ricci Armani, 13; Tel. 01 87 83 01 20; Category 2–3)*; The hotel-restaurant *Rustichello* in *Madonna del Monte* near Mulazzo *offers overnight accommodation (Open Fri–Sun, except May–Oct; 8 rooms; Tel. 01 87 43 97 59; Category 3).*

Marina di Carrara (104/B3–4)

❂ ✸ Has a beautiful yacht harbour. The *marble museum* in Marina di Carrara depicts the history of marble in several stages – its quarrying, working, and uses (*Open 10 am–5 pm daily in May; 10 am–8 pm June–Sept; 8.30 am–1.30 pm, Oct–April; Viale XX Settembre*). Located on the same avenue is the *Ristorante da Gero*, an exceptionally friend-ly establishment with excellent cuisine (*Closed Sun; Viale XX Settembre, 305; Tel. 058 55 52 55; Category 2*). *Marina di Massa* (a camper's paradise) and *Marina di Pietrasanta* are other sea-side resorts in the northern Ver-silia region. Wonderful sandy beaches, pine forests and many aquatic activities, but less expen-sive than elsewhere along the coast here.

Marble quarries (104/C3)

↘ The *cave* can be reached from Carrara on a well sign-posted road. Roadside stalls offering marble artefacts. In *Colonnata*, a former miners' colony, there is a *monument* on the main square to the miners themselves – made of marble. The *Locanda Apuana* is surprisingly comfortable and of-fers outstanding cuisine (*Closed Sun evening and Mon; Tel. 05 85 76 80 17; Category 2*); across the road in the *Galerie 'l Grup*, set against the background of the quarries, you can admire and purchase contemporary sculpture (*Open 10 am–12 midday and 4 pm–7 pm Wed–Mon; Tel. 05 85 76 80 03*). On the way to the marble quar-ries via *Fantiscritti* you come to the *Vara* bridges, built in the 19th century to allow the marble to be transported from the quar-ries. In the town itself there is a small *museum* (*variable opening hours; information at the souvenir shop opposite*), which provides a graphic insight into the process of marble quarrying.

Pietrasanta (104/C4)

Pietrasanta (pop. 25,000) is ac-tually located in the province of Lucca, but as in Massa and Car-rara, life here is governed by marble. The surrounding area, with its villas and olive groves, is not quite as steep and everything is less demanding. It is more the art of stoneworking than exhaus-ting quarry labour that has moulded the character of this city. Its focal point is the elong-ated ✪ *cathedral square* with the *Collegiata di S. Martino* (13th cen-tury) made entirely of marble (of course) and a brick campanile, flanked by the church of *S. Agostino* (12th century) constructed of light travertine stone. The for-mer monastery contains the *Museo dei Bozzetti*, showing drawings and models for sculp-tures (*Open 6 pm–8 pm and 9 pm–midnight Tue–Sun, 15 June–31 Aug; otherwise 2.30 pm–7 pm Tue–Fri and 2.30 pm–6 pm Sat*). The crenellated wall of the medieval *Rocca di Sala* closes off the square to the east. Marina di Pietrasanta also has the most discos on the coast.

PISA

☛ City Map on page 74

(114/C4–5) ✦At the foot of the gently sloping Pisan Mountains, the city (pop. 99,000) stretches along both sides of the broad Arno River, and is situated only 9 km from its mouth. Relics tes-tify to the fact that Pisa was a settlement as far back as the Li-gurian era (5th century B.C.). The city amassed great wealth and influence as a seafaring re-public in the Middle Ages. By the 9th century Pisa had already used its fleet to monopolize trade in the western Mediterranean as far as the Arabic empires. When this fleet was totally destroyed by the rival Genoans in 1284, Pisa's slow but certain demise set in and when the harbour began to silt up, the fate of the mighty republic was sealed. In 1406 Pisa also fell to Florence and the powerful Medici realm. The imposing palaces along the promenade on both sides of the river and many edifices in the narrow, winding alleyways of the inner city are an indication of the wealth and the glory of this former naval power and the subsequent years of flourishing trade under Florentine rule.

Modern Pisa is an important agricultural centre and has significant pharmaceutical and metal-working industries. The world-famous Vespa was designed and built here. During the last few years the city's economy has been increasingly based on service industries, trade and tourism in particular.

People joke that Pisa has the highest IQ in all Italy. And not without reason: one-third of the city's population are students. This prompted an American newspaper to write that Pisa was a 'campus the size of a city'. Pisa already had a major university back in the Middle Ages. Today its eleven faculties provide tuition to over 30,000 students. However, its elevated position among Italy's universities is due to its Scuola Normale Superiore, founded in 1813 and based on the Parisian model of education. Students for this elite university, which offers degrees in the Social and Natural Sciences,

are selected annually from throughout Italy.

The high concentration of young people is immediately obvious wherever you go in Pisa and makes for an especially lively city with a real campus atmosphere – but not on weekends or during the summer vacation, when the city is almost lifeless, as the students head home.

Visitors are constantly reminded of the fact that they are in one of the world's most renowned tourist meccas, especially in the northern part of the city surrounding the Campo dei Miracoli, the 'Field of Miracles'. It is here that one finds the gleaming white Duomo, the Baptistery, the Camposanto and the Campanile – the famous Leaning Tower. But don't just follow the yellow municipal signs. Instead, escape the never-ending flow of tourists by exploring the city on foot; its centre is small and the river makes orienting oneself an easy task.

SIGHTS

Apart from the Duomo, all sights and museums are closed on 1 January and 25 December.

Baptistery

★ This circular, white marble edifice was built from 1152–1284 as a replica of a church in Jerusalem. The plans were drawn up and building was initiated by Diotisalvi, but in 1278 Nicola Pisano took over its supervision, and later still this role was assumed by his son Giovanni, who is also responsible for the sculptures in the small

72

Gothic loggia. The designer of the unique cupola remains unknown, but this does nothing to dampen the rich echo which can be heard inside it. The exquisite, hexagonal marble pulpit by Nicola Pisano (1260), depicting scenes from the life of Christ, is supported by seven narrow porphyry columns and is the best example of Early Gothic sculpture to be found in Italy. *Open daily in summer from 8 am–7.40 pm; spring and autumn 9 am–5.40 pm; Winter 9 am–4.40 pm*

Campanile

★ The Leaning Tower is Pisa's hallmark. Construction of the 55-m bell tower was begun in 1173. The master builder has not been positively identified, but according to the latest research the plans can be ascribed to Gerardo di Gerardo. Construction was halted after the fourth level of columned galleries was completed, because the tower had already begun to lean somewhat precariously in a southerly direction as a result of its sandy footing. It was only in the mid 14th century that the belfry was added and the structure was finally completed. The tower now leans about 4.2 m. Although the inclination, which has been recorded annually since 1985, has become less rapid, the Soprintendenza dei Beni Culturali (Ministry of Culture) in Rome closed the tower to all visitors in January 1990. Until further notice, visitors will only be able to admire it from behind barricades and piles of building materials – no more peering gingerly from the smooth, angled marble galleries to the lawn far below.

Camposanto

This cemetery is separated from the cathedral square by a simple white, limestone wall. The main entrance is adorned by a tabernacle depicting the Madonna and Child surrounded by saints. It is the only decoration in this structure and was completed by members of Giovanni Pisano's school. The columned galleries contain ancient sarcophagi, and tombstones are set into the walls and floors. The most arresting decorations in the Camposanto were, however, the frescos from the 13th and 14th centuries which covered all the walls. But in July 1944 the Camposanto was severely damaged in a bombing raid. This resulted in molten lead pouring down from the ceiling and destroying most of these glorious artworks. Even after many years of painstaking restoration only a few were salvaged and they are now on show in a special exhibition, together with photographic documentation of the original frescos and their destruction. Before entering, ask at the gate whether most of the sarcophagi and gravestones are actually in their places or are elsewhere being restored. *Open daily in summer 8 am–7.40 pm; Spring and autumn 9 am–5.40 pm; Winter 9 am–4.40 pm*

Duomo

★ The largest Romanesque edifice in Pisa, it was begun in 1063 under the supervision of the master builders Buscheto and Rainaldo. This flurry of building activity followed decisive victories at sea and the cathedral was finally dedicated to the Mother of Christ in 1118. The church,

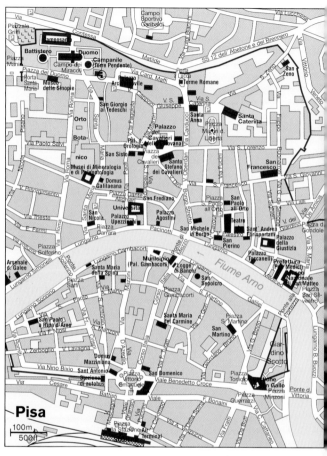

designed in the shape of a Latin cross, has a façade featuring 54 columns in four tiers and combines light and dark horizontal stripes of marble, lending the structure a bright, somewhat oriental feel reminiscent of Moorish architecture. The gable is crowned by a figure of the Madonna and Child by Nicola Pisano. The Portale di S. Ranieri, the bronze doors of the transept facing the Leaning Tower on the southern end, are by Bonanno Pisano (late 12th century). These doors lead to the tomb of the city's patron saint S. Ranieri, located in the right transept. They are the only doors to have escaped total destruction in the fire of 1595. The bronze portal of the main entrance is by members of the Giambologna School (16th century). The interior of the Romanesque basilica is dominated by the colossal figure of

Christ by Cimabue. The octagonal pulpit has marble reliefs by Giovanni Pisano and is considered to represent the pinnacle of Gothic sculpture in Italy. The movement of the bronze lamp suspended in the nave is said to have motivated Pisa's most famous son, Galileo Galilei, to develop his theories on the motion of pendulums. *Open 10 am–7.40 pm Mon–Sat, 1 pm–7.40 pm Sun; Winter 10 am–12.45 pm Mon–Sat, 3 pm–4.45 pm Sun*

Murales

A huge wall covered in classic designs by Keith Haring. *Piazza Vittorio Emanuele*

Orto Botanico

Created in 1543, the Botanical Garden is the oldest in the world. A good place to escape the crowds while admiring the wealth of vegetation. *Open 8 am–5.30 pm Mon–Fri; 8 am–1 pm Sat; Via Luca Ghini, 5*

Palazzo della Sapienza

The seat of the largest university in Pisa, construction began in 1472 and was completed in 1543 on the basis of plans by Brunelleschi. Established as a *studium generale* at the start of the 14th century and later sponsored by the Medici, the Palazzo della Sapienza still houses one of the most renowned universities in the world, with eleven faculties and over 30,000 students, whose presence is felt throughout the whole city. The old *Aula Magna* (portraits of former Pisan teachers) and the *inner courtyard* with its *loggias* are open to the public, but you have to ask the gatekeeper for admission. *Via XXIV Maggio*

Piazza dei Cavalieri

❖ Originally a Roman forum, it was remodelled in the mid 16th century by Giorgio Vasari. The centre of the square is dominated by the *Palazzo dei Cavalieri* with its beautiful black and white *sgraffito* decoration (designs scratched into wet plaster). Today it houses one of Pisa University's most prestigious colleges, the *Scuola Normale Superiore.* To the right is the church of *S. Stefano dei Cavalieri,* the principal church of the order of knights of the same name. On the left-hand side of the *Piazza* is the *Palazzo dell'Orologio* which incorporates the medieval town jail. The building now holds a library, but at one time it served as the hospital for the knights of S. Stefano. In 1288 it was the scene of terrible brutality, when the Mayor of Pisa, along with his sons and grandsons, were walled up there after being accused of treachery. Two expansive palaces complete the face of the square: the *Palazzo del Collegio Puteano* and the *Palazzo del Consiglio dell'Ordine dei Cavalieri di S. Stefano.*

Ponte di Mezzo

The oldest bridge in the city joins the suburbs of Mezzogiorno (in the south) and Tramontana (to the north of the river). Today the *Gioco del Ponte* and the *Regata di San Ranieri* are held here in summer. On the south bank lies the *Piazza XX Settembre* with the *Palazzo Gambacorti* built in 1369 (today it is the town hall) and the *Logge dei Banchi*, which was erected from 1603–05 as a market hall for silk and wool trading.

S. Caterina d'Alessandria

A church from the 13th century featuring a beautiful marble

rosette and works by Nicola and Nino Pisano. *Piazza S. Caterina*

S. Maria della Spina

A Gothic jewel on the southern bank of the Arno. The chapel was dismantled in 1872 when the river was straightened and rebuilt on the raised bank. According to legend a thorn from the Crown of Christ is kept in the interior shrine. Unfortunately, the church tends to be closed most of the time. *Lungarno Gambacorti*

S. Nicola

Really worth seeing for its gently leaning bell tower with an octagonal base. At a higher level it has 16 sides and it is encircled by a loggia. It is thought to have been designed by Nicola Pisano and is considered a masterpiece of medieval architecture. You can climb the open, spiral staircase to the bell tower, which is also a leaning tower. The interior has, among other things, a wooden cross and a figure of the Madonna and Child by Giovanni and Nino Pisano. *Via S. Maria*

S. Paolo a Ripa d'Arno

The façade is captivating as it appears to be a replica of the Duomo's façade in miniature. The Construction of the Romanesque-Tuscan basilica was begun in 805. Behind the church there is the small, octagonal prayer house of S. Agata (12th century). *Piazza S. Paolo a Ripa d'Arno*

S. Pietro in Vinculis

While Roman harbour structures provided the inspiration for the crypt, this basilica is especially impressive because of its elaborate mosaic floor. *Via Cavour*

Museo Nazionale di S. Matteo

The courtyard of this former monastery from the 13th century, in which the museum is housed, is surrounded on three sides by arcades. Its rooms hold over 500 pieces from the 13th and 14th centuries. There is also a fine collection of painted panels, wooden carved figures and ancient ceramics. *Open 9 am–7 pm Tue–Sat, 9 am–2 pm Sun; Closed 1 Jan, 1 May, 15 Aug and 25 Dec; Lungarno Mediceo*

Museo dell'Opera del Duomo

On display here are the treasures from the Duomo and the sculptures created for the Duomo and Baptistery by Nicola and Giovanni Pisano, as well as the relics and documents concerning the Duomo and the area surrounding it. *Open daily 8 am–8 pm; Winter 9 am–5 pm; Piazza Arcivescovado*

Museo delle Sinopie

On the southern side of the cathedral square lies an elongated brick building belonging to the Ospedale S. Chiara (1257). Here you can find the sketches for the frescos which no longer exist in the Camposanto. They were removed during restoration, so visitors still have an opportunity to admire this extensive collection of medieval drawings. *Open in summer 8 am–7.40 pm; Spring and autumn 9 am–5.40 pm; Winter 9 am–12.40 pm and 3 pm–4.40 pm*

Antica Trattoria da Bruno

In summer you can dine outside at this establishment serving excellent local cuisine. *Closed Mon*

evening and Tue; Via Bianchi, 12;
Tel. 050 56 08 18; Category 2

Banco della Berlina

A venue for night owls: It opens
in the evening and remains so
until the early hours of the
morning. Closed Mon; Piazza dei
Facchini, 13; Tel. 05 02 84 61;
Category 3

Kostas

Not only the seafood and meat
dishes but also the vegetarian
meals are extremely good here.
Closed Sun midday and Mon; Via del
Borghetto, 39; Tel. 050 57 14 67;
Category 3

Al Ristoro dei Vecchi Macelli

'In the old abattoir', as it is known
in Italian, is one of the best
restaurants in Pisa, with air conditioning in summer and some
outdoor seating. Closed Sun midday and Wed; Via Volturno, 49; Tel.
05 02 04 24; Category 1–2

Lo Schiaccianoci

For years the 'Nutcracker' has
been an exceptionally popular restaurant in Pisa. Try the fine fish
dishes! Closed Sun; Via Amerigo
Vespucci, 104; Tel. 05 02 10 24;
Category 2

Turrido

Lunchtime or evening wood-
fired pizza. Closed Sun; Piazza
S. Frediano, 12; Category 3

SHOPPING

Every other weekend there is an
✪ antiques market in the streets
surrounding the Piazza XX Settembre at the southern end of the
Ponte di Mezzo. Under the
arches of the Borgo Stretto you
will discover the finest shops in
the city. There are also two of
Pisa's best cake shops, the Pasticceria Bagnani and the Pasticceria
Salza, serving the tastiest in typical Pisan bakery products and
sweets. You can either take them
away or enjoy them with a cappuccino under the arches. With
children's fashion at discounts of
up to 50 per cent, both parents
and grandparents alike will find
it hard to resist having a browse
in Baby Stockeria (Via Turati, 4)

ACCOMMODATION

Hotel Ariston

Reasonably priced, mid-range
hotel right on the cathedral
square. Facilities for the disabled. 48 rooms; Via Maffi, 42; Tel.
050 56 18 34; Fax 050 56 18 91;
Category 3

Jolly Hotel Cavalieri

First-class hotel, not quiet, but
conveniently located opposite
the station and airport terminal.
100 rooms; Piazza della Stazione, 2;
Tel. 05 04 32 90; Fax 050 50 22 42;
Category 1

Ostello della Gioventù
Residence Madonna dell'Acqua

This modern complex, which
houses a youth hostel, student
dormitory and hostel all under
one roof, lies 1 km from the
centre (bus). Via Pietrasantina, 15;
Tel. and Fax 050 89 06 22 (6 pm–9
pm daily); Category 3

Hotel Royal Victoria

Dignified splendour on the
banks of the Arno with 48 large
and attractive rooms. Lungarno
Pacinotti, 12; Tel. 050 94 01 11;
Fax 050 94 01 80; Category 2

ENTERTAINMENT

In summer the cathedral square *(Piazza dei Miracoli)* and the surrounding parks are popular places to meet for a chat and an ice-cream. Other spots include *Harvard's Bar (Closed Sat; Via S. Maria, 95)* and *La Tazza d'Oro (Closed Sun; Piazza Clari, 2).*

INFORMATION

Piazza Duomo, 56126 Pisa; Tel. 050 56 04 64; Fax 05 04 09 03

SURROUNDING AREA

Calci   (115/D–E4–5)

Twelve km to the east, situated on the slopes of the Pisan Mountains in the vicinity of Calci there is a Carthusian monastery founded in the middle of the 14th century, the *Certosa di Pisa.* Carefully restored in the 17th and 18th centuries, today it constitutes one of the most impressive Baroque ensembles in Tuscany. The church, monastery courtyards, Grand Ducal guest wing and the lovely park are all open to the public *(Open 9 am–7 pm Tue–Sun; 9 am–1 pm Sun; Closed 1 Jan, 1 May and 25 Dec).* In 1994 the *Museo di Storia Naturale e del Territorio* was established in one wing of the monastery *(Open Sept–June: 9 am–6 pm Tue–Sun; July: 4 pm–midnight Tue, Thu and Sat; Aug: 4 pm–midnight Tue–Sat, 10 am–1 pm Sun; Closed 1–10 June, 18, 25, 31 Dec and 1 Jan).* The Museum of Natural Science includes a rich collection assembled by Ferdinand I de'Medici which was previously the property of the University of Pisa; the skeleton collection is world-renowned.

In the town of Calci itself there is the baptismal church of *Pieve S. Giovanni Evangelista e S. Ermolao Martire.* The squat bell tower and the façade encrusted with black and white marble were never completed, but they provide an insight into the significance of this village church (11th century). The nave and two aisles with their ancient columns have been modified often. The most significant work of art is the baptismal font sculpted from a single marble block. Its reliefs portray the baptism of Christ (12th century).

Marina di Pisa   (114/A–B5)

Popular around the turn of the century, this seaside town is directly at the mouth of the Arno, so swimming can't really be recommended. Along the boardwalk there are some good seafood restaurants.

Parco Regionale di Migliarino, S. Rossore e Massaciuccoli   (114/B2–5)

These 23,000 hectares of swampland with pine and oak forests, extending from Viareggio in the north, the Canale dei Navicelli in the south and inland towards the Tenuta di Coltano, were declared a national park in 1979. The heart of the park is the *S. Rossore* domain, once the hunting reserve of Italian kings and today under the control of the national president. This large park, with magnificent avenues and a rich variety of game, can be visited every weekend from 9 am to sunset. There are guided tours on foot, horseback, by bike and in horse-drawn vehicles on Tuesday, Thursday, Saturday and Sunday *(Information: Tel. 050 52 52 11; Fax 050 53 36 50; Entrance on Viale delle Cascine/Via Aurelia).* On the west bank of the *Lago di Massaciuccoli* lies the villa in which Giacomo Puccini composed several of his operas and where he is also buried. In summer the Festival Pucciniano is held on the shores of the lake, featuring opera productions *(Torre del Lago; Tel. 05 84 35 93 22; Fax 05 84 35 02 77).*

Riviera della Versilia (104/B–C3–5)

The coast from north of Pisa to La Spezia is notable for its gentle, sandy beaches and its elegant bathing facilities. You get a magnificent view over the entire coast from the ◆✷ veranda of the *Ristorante Il Vignaccio* in *S. Lucia* below Camaiore *(Open in summer only in the evening; Closed Wed; Tel. 05 84 91 42 00; Category 2).* Protected from the wind by the Apuan Alps, this coastal stretch became a meeting place for the gentry and artists alike throughout the entire year at around the turn of the century and is still considered to be one of the most elegant bathing spots in Tuscany today.

San Giuliano Terme (115/D4)

Both Byron and Shelley sought treatment for their liver ailments in these 40°C (104°F) thermal springs. Not far away in *Rigoli* is the stylistically nostalgic *Villa di Corliano* from the 16th and 17th centuries, situated in an expansive, partially overgrown park *(13 rooms; Tel. 050 81 81 93; Fax 050 81 88 97; Category 2).*

San Piero a Grado (114/B5)

The spot where the small, exquisite Romanesque *basilica* of *S. Piero a Grado (Open 9 am–12 midday and 3 pm–7 pm Mon–Sat; 7.30–1 pm and 3 pm–7 pm Sun)* stands today was once Pisa's harbour. According to legend this is the place where in 44 A.D. St. Peter came ashore on his way to Rome. Exceptionally well-maintained frescos from the 13th and 14th centuries depict the legend of St. Peter.

Tirrenia (114/B6)

◆✷ Broad, sandy beach and much activity, as well as two golf courses. The *Grand Hotel Golf* is open the whole year round and has facilities for the disabled. It also has a beautiful park, tennis courts, sauna and a heated swimming pool *(77 rooms; Tel. 05 03 75 45; Fax 05 03 21 11; Category 1–2).* There are also several less expensive establishments. *Information: Tel. 05 03 25 10*

Viareggio (114/A2)

The most renowned and frequented seaside resort (pop. 58,000) along the Versilia, this city is simply inundated by tourists in the thousands during the summer months. It is known for its palm-lined avenues, *fin-de-siècle* buildings *(Grand Caffè Margherita)*, elegant boutiques and restaurants, such as the *L'Oca Bianca (Closed midday and Tue; Via Coppino, 409; Tel. 05 84 38 84 77; Category 1)* and the *Romano* with its one Michelin star *(Closed Mon; Via Mazzini, 120; Tel. 058 43 13 82; Category 1).* The yacht harbour is one of the most popular on the Mediterranean and its yacht-building yard is the second largest in the world. The end of July sees the Viareggio–Bastia sailing regatta set off from here. In February there are massive carnival processions, but the depots with the carriages can also be viewed in summer *(Hangar Carnevale, Viale Marco Polo).*

Provinces with a past

*Mountains and sweeping plains mark the landscape
around Lucca and Pistoia*

Northern Tuscany encompasses an area which includes Florence, the lower Arno valley and the provinces of Prato, Pistoia, Lucca, including their respective capitals, and parts of the province of Massa-Carrara.

LUCCA

(115/D–E2) ★ One of the most significant historical cities in Tuscany, Lucca is situated on the lower reaches of the Serchio River in what was previously a swamp at the base of the Apuan Alps, which rise in a northerly direction. The city (pop. 87,000) is enclosed by a massive 4.2-km brick wall, which is 12 m tall and just as wide at the base. Eleven bastions (previously 12) strengthen it at strategically important locations. Today you can walk along these ⚘ *tree-lined ramparts* . This defensive structure, built in the years between 1544 and 1645, guaranteed the city's independence until 1847, when it joined the duchy of Tuscany – and also saved the city many times from the flood waters of the Serchio.

As is the case with most cities in Tuscany, Lucca was founded in pre-Roman times. The city was of particular significance in the Middle Ages as a stopover point on the Via Francigena, the major Franconian road joining Rome with northern Europe. Lucca became an independent city republic back in 1369 and and remained the only city in Tuscany which never succumbed to the power of the Medici. At the beginning of the 19th century the city was subject to a strong French influence when Napoleon declared Lucca a principality. The influence of French architectural styles is especially visible around the Piazza del Giglio.

Since the early Middle Ages Lucca's wealth has been generated by the production of and trade in precious materials, even though today agricultural trade from the surrounding area has become its most important asset. The outskirts of the city have been totally overdeveloped, with

*Piazza San Michele,
the centre of Lucca, at a
quiet moment*

MARCO POLO SELECTION: THE NORTH

1 Uffizi in Florence
Florence is a must, and when there visit the Uffizi Galleries - when the huge crowds recede a little (page 30)

2 Montecatini Terme
Elegant spa experience in a nostalgic Belle Epoque setting (page 89)

3 Vinci
Leonardo's birthplace and museum with displays of his designs and inventions (page 91)

4 Lucca
A beautiful medieval city and ideal starting point for hiking trips to the Garfagnana and Apuan Alps (page 81)

5 Grotta del Vento
At 3,500 metres, Europe's longest limestone caves with stalactites and stalagmites, near Fornovolasco (page 86)

6 Prato
The Centro per l'Arte Contemporanea Luigi Pecci should not be missed by any lover of modern art (page 91)

the remaining magnificent villas looking somewhat out of place. Thankfully, the inner-city has been barred to traffic so that its historical buildings can be enjoyed in relative peace.

SIGHTS

Dom S. Martino

Construction began in the 6th century and continued right through to the 13th century. Restoration work was carried out in the 14th and 15th centuries, and again for the last time in the 19th century, lending the façade a mixture of styles. The basilica contains some quite exceptional treasures. The *Volto Santo*, the Holy Visage, a wooden crucifix with a bearded Christ on an almost black background of Lebanon cedar, is said to have been carved by St. Nicodemus at the time of the crucifixion and

brought to Lucca in 782. Every year on 13 September the decorated relic is carried in a procession through the candlelit city. For the remainder of the year it rests in a small shrine in the fourth bay on the left of the nave. The altar by Giambologna is decorated with a relief depicting Lucca in the 16th century. The sacristy holds a magnificent Renaissance tomb. Its marble sarcophagus was completed by Jacopo della Quercia in 1408 in commemoration of Ilaria di Carretto, who died in labour. She was the youthful wife of Paolo Guinigi, Lucca's ruling lord at the time.

Piazza del Mercato

❖ The remarkable elliptical shape of this former Roman amphitheatre is bounded by 3-to-5-storey buildings which house many fine shops under the 56 arches of the arcades. These boutiques can be accessed either directly from the Piazza or from the street to their rear.

Piazza Napoleone

Encircled by sycamores, this Piazza has real French flair. It was designed by a French garden planner in 1799 under instruction from Napoleon's sister, Elisa Baciocchi. She was later appointed as the city's ruler from 1805 to 1815. The statue on the square, however, is of her successor, Marie Louise de Bourbon. Directly accessible from this square is the *Piazza del Giglio* with its beautiful *theatre* of the same name from the 18th century.

Piazza S. Michele

The highlight of this medieval square, situated on the site of an ancient Roman forum, is the church of S. Michele in Foro (12th century). The façade has five tiers and every column is uniquely sculptured. Figures include a prince being crowned by a statue of the Archangel Michael flanked by two dragons. The Madonna illuminated by carved rays of light on the left-hand side of the façade was added in 1480 after the plague had run its murderous course.

S. Frediano

This basilica is from the 6th century. One shrine contains St. Zita, the patron saint of Lucca, and the Madonna, as well as a famous mosaic depicting the Ascension of Christ (early 13th century) which adorns the narrow façade.

S. Giovanni e Reparata

The remnants of a cathedral from the 1st century B.C. and an early Christian church can be viewed inside this impressive Romanesque basilica and its baptistery. *Open 10 am–6 pm Mon–Fri (Nov–Mar 10 am–2 pm), 10 am–5 pm Sat and Sun*

San Michele in Foro with its almost 50 unique columns

Via Fillungo

✪ The main commercial thoroughfare in Lucca, this well-preserved example of a medieval street lined with towers and palaces runs from the Church of S. Cristoforo along the Piazza del Mercato to the Piazza S. Maria. It is also very popular for shopping and strolling.

Casa Natale di Giacomo Puccini

This is of particular interest to music fans from around the globe. The birthplace of Giacomo Puccini, the house contains displays of various keepsakes belonging to this famous Italian composer of operatic works. *Open 15 Mar–15 Nov, Tue–Sun 10 am–1 pm and 3 pm–6 pm; 16 Nov–31 Dec 10 am–1 pm only; 1 Jan–14 Mar only groups of 15* people or more (Bookings Tel. 05 83 34 16 12); Via di Poggio, Corte S. Lorenzo, 9

Museo Palazzo Controni Pfanner

Since 1980 the Piano Nobile of this palace from the 17th century has housed an interesting museum containing materials and costumes from the 18th to 20th centuries. Unfortunately, only the delightful garden can be viewed at present. *Open daily 10 am–6 pm Mar–Oct; Via degli Asili, 33*

Museo Nazionale di Palazzo Mansi

In addition to the major paintings and artworks from the 16th to 19th centuries, the palace itself and its original interior fittings (18th century) can also be admired. Lucca's local silk weaving industry is well documented in a separate exhibition. *Open 9 am–7 pm Tue–Sat, 9 am–2 pm Sun; Closed 1 Jan, 1 May and 25 Dec; Via Galli Tassi, 43*

Museo Nazionale di Villa Guinigi

The original treasures in this museum housed in the restored Guinigi family palace (15th century) came from disbanded churches and monasteries in the 18th century. Most pieces are sculptures created between the 8th and 16th centuries. *Open 9 am-7 pm Tue-Sat, 9 am-2 pm Sun; Closed 1 Jan, 1 May and 25 Dec; Via della Quarquonia*

RESTAURANTS

Antica Locanda dell'Angelo

Elegant and comfortable, it is situated close to the Piazza Napoleone. *Closed Sun evening and Mon; Via Pescheria, 21; Tel. 058 34 77 11; Category 2*

Buca di Sant'Antonio

A former stopover for mail coaches, it serves fine Luccan cuisine. *Closed Sun evening and Mon; Via della Cervia, 3; Tel. 058 35 58 81; Category 2*

Da Giulio in Pelleria

Located in the former tanning quarter in the vicinity of the Porta S. Tommaso, this *trattoria* has hearty local fare. *Closed Sun and Mon; Via delle Conce, 47; Tel. 058 35 59 48; Category 3*

Da Leo

❂ This typical Luccan *trattoria* is always full and offers all the local specialities. *Closed Sun; Via Tegrimi, 1; Tel. 05 83 49 22 36; Category 3*

Ristorante La Mora

〰〰 A very traditional establishment with a lovely verandah and magnificent views, its cuisine is considered to be as good as any to be had in Tuscany. *Closed Wed; Suburb of Ponte a Moriano; Tel. 05 83 40 64 02; Category 1–2*

Ristorante Solferino

Its meals are excellent (also served in the garden in summer) and you can buy local olive oil and tasty sheep's milk cheese (*pecorino*) to take away. *Closed Wed; Suburb of S. Macario in Piano (about 6 km in the direction of the coast); Tel. 05 83 591 18; Category 2*

Ristorante Vipore

〰〰 Delicious meals served in an old farmhouse with a lovely view of the landscape and a nice garden. *Closed Mon and midday, except Sat and Sun; Suburb of Pieve S. Stefano; Tel. 058 35 92 45; Category 2*

SHOPPING

You can't leave Lucca without visiting the traditional ❖ *Caffè Di Simo* with its famous liqueurs (*Via Fillungo, 58*). There are silk gobelins (tapestries) at *Luisa Raffaelli, Via Anfiteatro, 15* and *Mamma Rò* sells lovely ceramics at No. 4. On the third weekend of every month on the ❖ *Piazza S. Martino* there is an *antiques market*.

ACCOMMODATION

Ostello del Serchio (youth hostel)
Closed Nov–Feb; Via del Brennero (Bus 7 from the station); Tel. and Fax 05 83 34 18 11

San Marco
Totally modern with air conditioning, subterranean parking and an impressive breakfast. *42 rooms; Via S. Marco, 368; Tel. 05 83 49 50 10; Fax 05 83 49 05 13; Category 2*

Hotel Universo
Refined establishment near the Piazza Napoleone opposite the theatre. Good restaurant (*Closed Thu*). *61 rooms; Piazza del Giglio, 1; Tel. 05 83 49 36 78; Fax 05 83 95 48 54; Category 1–2*

Villa Casanova
10 km to the west in a delightfully situated, 18th-century farmstead; simple but cosy, with thermal pool, leisure activities and good food. *40 rooms; Balbano-Nozzano; Tel. 05 83 54 84 29; Fax 05 83 36 89 55; Category 3*

Villa La Principessa
Situated in a magnificent park, this former country residence of the Bourbon-Parma was built in the 18th century. Restaurant *(Closed Sun). 40 rooms; Closed Nov–Mar; Massa Pisana (6 km in the direction of Pisa); Tel. 05 83 37 97 37; Fax 05 83 37 90 19; Category 1*

ENTERTAINMENT

Starting in September you can attend performances at the *Teatro del Giglio (Bookings Tel. 058 34 61 47)* or spend time at the ❖ *Antico Caffè delle Mura* (also a restaurant) near the Porta S. Pietro on the ramparts *(Closed Tue; Via Vittorio Emanuele; Category 1–2)*. The cool place to be seen is *Mirò*, with its huge range of cocktails and great music *(Closed Mon; Via de'Fossi, 215; Category 2)*.

INFORMATION

Piazzale Verdi, 55100 Lucca; Tel. 05 83 41 96 89; Fax 05 83 49 07 66

Club Alpino Italiano (CAI)
Information for mountain climbers and hikers. *Open 7 pm–8 pm Mon–Sat; Palazzo Ducale, Cortile Carrara; Tel. 05 83 58 26 69*

SURROUNDING AREA

Barga (105/D3)
◁▷ This town (pop. 10,000) is situated on a mountain peak (great view) and has beautiful Romanesque *Duomo* and medieval alleys and buildings. An *opera festival* takes place in July and on the first weekend of August there is also a highly amusing *donkey race*.

Coreglia Antelminelli (105/D3)
This little town near Barga is worth the short detour for its *Museo della Figurina di Gesso e dell'Emigrazione*, a unique collec-

tion of plaster casts and nativity figures *(Open in summer 8 am–1 pm Mon-Sat, 10 am–1 pm and 4 pm–7 pm; in winter 8 am–1 pm Mon-Sat; Palazzo Vanni).*

Garfagnana (104/C3, 105/D3–4)

You can reach this unexpectedly interesting region of Tuscany by driving up through the Serchio River valley. On the left you drive past the rocky cliffs of the Apuan Alps and on the right the chestnut-covered slopes of the Garfagnana, the western foothills of the Appenines. The Garfagnana is a great place to go hiking at any time of the year and there are many well-signposted walking tracks maintained by the Italian Alpine Association (CAI). At the bottom end of the valley on the eastern side you can see the famous Luccan villas, the *Villa Reale* in *Marlia*, former country residence of Napoleon's sister Elisa Baciocchi *(only guided tours of the park)*, and near *Segromino* the *Villa Mansi (Villa and park can be viewed)* and the *Villa Torrigiani* in *Camigliano (in winter only open Sun)*. A road to the right leads past the *Borgo a Mozzano* with its *Devil's Bridge* from the 12th century, which elegantly spans the Serchio River to *Bagni di Lucca*. There are 19 springs at this health spa set amidst thick chestnut forests, with the 38°–54°C (70°–130°F) radioactive sulphuric water used for bathing and medicinal purposes. In summer there is also a hot outdoor pool. This health spa resort from the turn of the century is located in the valley. *(Open April–Nov; Information: Tel. 058 38 79 46).* Pleasant *fin-de-siècle* atmosphere at the *Hotel Roma (Closed Oct–April; Tel. and Fax 058 38 72 78; Fine cuisine at Ristorante del Sonno, both Category 3).*

From Gallicano at the foot of the valley, a narrow road heads off in a westerly direction through a valley with a raging torrent toward Fornovolasco and to the entrance to the imposing ★ *Grotta del Vento*, a 3,500-m limestone cave with stalagmites and stalactites, the longest in Europe *(Open daily April–Sept and in winter on Sat and Sun; Guided tours of 1–3 hours from 10 am–6 pm; Tel. 05 83 72 20 24 – don't forget to bring warm clothes).* From Castelnuovo di Garfagnana a road via Corfino leads to the *Orechiella nature reserve* situated at an altitude of 1,200 m. A very windy but beautiful stretch of road (SS324) circumvents the Garfagnana and takes you to Lucca on the SS12 via Abetone and S. Marcello Pistoiese – a great day trip through enchanting countryside.

If you stay on the SS445 through the Serchio Valley you drive through Giuncagno Varliano (876 m) to reach *Aulla* in the Magra Valley.

PISTOIA

(116/C1, 117/D1) Founded around 200 B.C., its geographically and strategically advantageous location between Monte Albano in the south and the steep mountains of the Appenines in the north (dissected by the Via Cassia) has aided the development of the city since Roman times. The largest tree nurseries in Europe, important metalworking businesses and mechanical engineering workshops have made this province one of the wealthiest in Tuscany.

Pistoia (pop. 88,000) is a good place to base yourself for trips and hiking expeditions into the Pistoian Mountains to the north.

The best way to see the historic old city is by bike. You can borrow one at no charge at the *Piazza Monteoliveto* and at the *Piazza della Resistenza* .

SIGHTS

Giardino Zoologico
✽ The local zoo, which is well-presented and has many exhibits in a delightful setting, is found on the western outskirts of the city. *Open daily April–Sept 9 am–7 pm, Oct–Mar 9 am–5 pm; Via di Pieve a Celle, 160*

Ospedale del Ceppo with the Museo dei Ferri Chirurgici
The façade of the ancient plague hospice (13th century) is decorated with a colourful terracotta frieze by the Della Robbia brothers. Inside there is an unusual museum exhibiting surgical instruments from throughout the ages. *Entry only by appointment; Tel. 05 73 35 22 09; Viale Matteotti, 19*

Piazza del Duomo
This square is the focal point of the historic, annular city centre. Located here are the *Duomo S. Zeno* (12th century), containing a silver altar on which goldsmiths worked from 1287–1456, its columned *Campanile* and the octagonal *Baptistery*, which is also in Pisan-Gothic style with green-and-white marble cladding (after plans by Andrea Pisano). The medieval *Palazzo Comunale* houses the *Museo Civico*. On Wednesday and Saturday mornings a lively ✪ *weekly market* is held on the cathedral square.

S. Andrea
Has the first marble pulpit by Giovanni Pisano, which he completed in 1301.

MUSEUMS

Centro di Documentazione e Fondazione Marino Marini
Documentation centre with drawings, sculptures, and lithographs by the Pistoian artist Marino Marini (1901–1980). *Open 9 am–1 pm and 3 pm–7 pm Tue–Sat, 9 am–12.30 pm Sun; Palazzo del Tau, Corso S. Fedi*

Museo Civico and Centro di Documentazione Giovanni Michelucci
Here one finds wood panels and sculptures by masters of the Pistoian and Florentine Schools from the 13th to 18th centuries, as well as furniture and small artworks. The second floor has a permanent exhibition of contemporary art (1930–1980) and a documentation centre for Giovanni Michelucci (1891–1990), a pioneer of modern Italian architecture. *Open 10 am–7 pm Tue–Sat, 9 am–12.30 pm Sun; Palazzo Comunale, Piazza del Duomo*

Nuovo Museo Diocesano
You can view a couple of the chambers occupied by Pope Clemens IX in the 17th century and also religious treasures from the diocese. *Open 10 am–1 pm and 4 pm–7 pm Tue, Thu and Fri; 10 am–1 pm Wed and Sat; Palazzo Rospigliosi, Via Ripa del Sale, 3*

Museo di S. Zeno and Percorso Archeologico Attrezzato
The old 12th-century bishop's palace contains a display of beau-

tiful treasures from the cathedral. The foundation of the building is of particular interest as it is set on Roman and pre-Roman buildings. The various architectural eras are described on informative panels along an 'archeological path' with reference to artefacts found in the area. *Viewing only as part of a guided tour; 8.30 am, 10 am, 11.30 am and 3.30 pm Tue, Thu and Fri; also 2.30 pm and 4.45 pm Fri (Tel. 05 73 36 92 72; Bookings advisable), Piazza Duomo*

RESTAURANTS

Il Castagno

Gourmet restaurant in a beautiful setting which also offers overnight accommodation. *Only open evenings (apart from Sun) and closed Mon; Suburb of Castagno di Piteccio; Tel. and Fax 057 34 22 14; Category 2*

Osteria del Contadino

Situated in the village of Agliana, between Pistoia and Prato, is the 'Farmers Osteria' – actually a top-class restaurant. *Closed all day Mon, also Tue and Wed evenings; Via Provinciale Pratese; Tel. 05 74 71 84 50; Category 2*

La Cugna

9 km towards Bologna on the SS 64. Truck drivers all stop here – a good indication of hearty fare. There are tables outside in summer. *Closed Wed; Via Bolognese, 236, Suburb of Corbezzi; Tel. 05 73 47 50 00; Category 2–3*

Pasticceria la Sala

Snacks and sweets in a nostalgic café with a view over the market. *Closed Wed; Piazza della Sala, 14–15*

Lo Storno

Popular meeting place serving local specialities in the vicinity of the cathedral. *Closed Mon–Wed evenings and Sun; Via del Lastrone, 8; Tel. 057 32 61 93; Category 3*

SHOPPING

The centre of town has exclusive boutiques, purveying fashion and antiques in particular. In the ❂ *Breda halls* there is an *antique market* every second weekend.

ACCOMMODATION

Il Convento

❧ Located in a former monastery, it is set on a mountain slope with a great view, pool and restaurant. *23 rooms; Via S. Quirico, 33, Pontenuovo; Tel. 05 73 45 26 51; Fax 05 73 45 35 78; Category 2*

Patria

Situated against the city walls, but has no restaurant. *28 rooms; Via Crispi, 6; Tel. 057 32 51 87; Fax 05 73 36 81 68; Category 3*

Piccolo Ritz

Italy's leading designers have done their utmost to make a guest's (and their dog's) stay a memorable one. *21 rooms; Via A. Vannucci, 67; Tel. 057 32 67 75; Fax 057 32 77 98; Category 3*

INFORMATION

Palazzo dei Vescovi, Via Roma, 1, 51100 Pistoia; Tel. 057 32 16 22; Fax 057 33 43 27

SURROUNDING AREA

Abetone   (105/E3)

❧ ✦ Climatic health and winter sport resort on a 1,388-m mountain ridge with forests, hiking tracks and groomed ski slopes. Hotels of every standard and a *youth hostel, the Ostello della Gioventù (Open 20 Dec–31 Mar and 15 June–30 Sept; Via Brennero, 157; Tel. 057 36 01 17). Information: Piazzale delle Piramidi, 51021 Abetone; Tel. 057 36 02 31; Fax 057 36 02 32*

Cerreto Guidi (116/C4)

Cosimo I had this massive villa with broad ramped steps built according to plans by Buontalenti in 1557. The villa is connected to the Church of S. Leonardo (13th century) by a gallery. *Open 9 am–7 pm Mon–Sat, 9 am–2 pm Sun*

Collodi (115/F1)

Park, castle, village: This is the sequence up the hill in the village of Collodi as one ascends the ridge. Carlo Lorenzini (Collodi) made it famous by writing his story about a puppet named Pinocchio here in 1880. The figures in the *Pinocchio Park* and various rooms in *Garzoni Castle* will seem very familiar to his readers. *Castle gardens and Pinocchio Park open daily 9 am–4 pm*

Empoli (117/D5)

Located at the lower end of the Arno Valley on the Pisa–Florence motorway, this industrial city (glass production) goes back to Roman times and has a well-preserved medieval city centre (pop. 44,000). Buildings of major significance are the church of *Collegiata di S. Andrea* built in 1093 and the *museum* of the same name with its impressive panels and statues by Tuscan artists from the 14th to 18th centuries. *(Open 9 am–12 midday Tue–Sun, also 4 pm–7 pm Thu–Sun).* The church of *S. Stefano* has lovely frescos by Masolino.

Medici villas (117/E3)

The two most beautiful are *La Ferdinanda (viewing after prior booking; Tel. 05 58 79 20 30 and 05 58 71 80 81)* above the village of *Artimino* and *Villa Ambra* near *Poggio a Caiano (Open daily Nov–Feb 9 am–3.30 pm; Mar and Oct 9 am–4.30 pm; April, May and Sept 9 am–5.30 pm; June–Aug 9 am–6.30 pm; Closed every 2nd and 3rd Mon of the month).* They are only a couple of kilometres apart in the vicinity of the Strada Statale 66 between Florence and Pistoia. Villa Ambra is surrounded by a particularly pretty park, and in the ⬆ page house of the villa in Artimino, high above the Arno Valley, there is a four-star hotel with an excellent restaurant *(Closed Wed and Thu midday)* and facilities for the disabled. *(Paggeria Medicea, 37 rooms; Artimino; Tel. 05 58 71 80 81; Fax 05 58 71 80 80; Category 1).*

Monsummano Terme (116/B2)

Medieval town in the Nievole Valley with probably the most renowned natural sauna in Italy. The *Grotta Giusti* extends 300 m into the mountain and has temperatures between 27°–35°C (81°–95°F) at 90 per cent humidity, making it a perfect therapeutic centre for those with rheumatic illnesses. The season is from April–November. The resort facilities *(Tel. 057 25 13 94)* are located in a lovely, wooded area. *Hotel: Grotta Giusti; Closed Dec–Feb; Facilities for the disabled; 70 rooms; Tel. 057 25 11 65; Fax 057 25 12 69; Category 2*

Montecatini Terme (116/B2)

★ The most famous and elegant of all thermal spas in Tuscany, it offers a range of treatments,

Assembly hall at Montecatini Terme

including those for liver complaints. The *fin-de-siècle* architecture of its pump rooms are impressive, as are the Belle Epoque hotels set in expansive parks and gardens. And of course the spa facilities more than measure up to international standards. There are nostalgic street cafés, not only along the spa resort boulevard, but also in the suburb of *Montecatini Alto* (situated further up the slope and with a quaint Piazza), which you reach by taking the funicular (a 10-minute ride). Montecatini Terme (pop. 21,000) has a large selection of hotels and restaurants in various price categories. One of the finest is the *Gourmet (Closed Tue; Viale Amendola, 6; Tel. 05 72 77 10 12; Category 1)*. There are also trotting races, concerts and auctions twice a week. *Information from the APT, Viale Verdi, 66 a, 51016 Montecatini Terme; Tel. 05 72 77 22 44; Fax 057 27 01 09*

Mugello   (106/A–B4)

Wealthy Florentine families built their castles here in the charming Sieve Valley to the north of the city back in the Middle Ages, seeking protection from the cold Apennine winds. The Medici came from *Trebbio Castle.* In 1451 Cosimo the Elder had *Cafaggiolo Castle* converted by Michelangelo. Both buildings lie close to the road from S. Piero a Sieve to Barberino di Mugello. In *S. Piero* itself there is the wonderful *Hotel La Felicina (10 rooms; Restaurant closed Fri; Tel. 05 58 49 81 81; Fax 05 58 49 81 57; Category 3, Restaurant Category 2)*. The main centre in Mugello is *Borgo S. Lorenzo* with its pretty baptismal church *(pieve)*. The largest agricultural ✪ *market* in Mugello is held here on the last weekend in May every year.

Prato   (117/E–F2)

When it comes to their neighbours, the Florentines love to quote the ambiguous saying 'All rags end up in Prato'. This not only refers to the fact that since the Middle Ages Prato's wealth has been accumulated by trading, sorting and reworking disused cloth from around the world, but also to the fact that this form of commerce has attracted many liberal thinkers to the city (pop. 166,000), which inspired its citizens to be very critical. Curzio Malaparte, Prato's disrespectful son, wrote his novel *Maledetti Toscani* while staying in the *Stella d'Italia*, a lovely old-fashioned hotel with a terrace overlooking the cathedral square. *(17 rooms; Piazza Duomo, 8; Tel. 057 42 79 10; Fax 057 44 02 89; Category 3)*. The *Art Hotel Museo (110 rooms; Viale della Repubblica, 289; Tel. 05 74 57 87; Fax 05 74 57 88 80; Category 1)* is extremely modern with swimming pool, sauna, tennis court and fine restaurant.

The Pratese have always been open to new artistic trends and at the *Teatro Metastasio (Via Verdi; Tel. 05 74 60 84)*, built in 1827 and considered one of the best theatres in Italy, some of the earliest avant-garde plays were performed. Today, contemporary pieces are also produced at the ✝ *Teatro Il Fabbricone (Viale Galilei; Tel. 05 74 69 09 62)*. The largest and most beautiful museum of contemporary art in Italy, the ★ *Centro per l'Arte Contemporanea Luigi Pecci (Open 10 am–7 pm Wed–Mon; Viale della Repubblica, 277)*, exhibits contemporary international art from recent years both in an open-air gallery measuring some 12,000 square metres and in ten large rooms. Significant artworks from the 14th to 18th centuries are to be found in the *Palazzo Pretorio (Closed at present for renovations)* and the *Museo di Pittura Murale opened in 1988 (Open 10 am–1 pm and 3.30 pm–7 pm Wed–Mon, 10 am–1 pm Sun; Piazza S. Domenico)*. The *Castello dell'Imperatore*, a fort from around 1000 A.D., was built by the Hohenstaufen emperor Friedrich II in 1237 in its current form. There are significant frescos in the churches of *S. Maria delle Carceri* and *S. Francesco* and also in the *Duomo*. In the right-hand corner of the cathedral façade there is a pulpit (with a relief by Donatello depicting cherubs) from which the cloak of the Virgin Mary is shown *(Il Sacro Cingolo)* on public holidays.

In the ✿ medieval city centre *(a pedestrian mall)* there are boutiques, nostalgic cafés *(Brogi on the Duomo square)* and cosy restaurants. The elegant *Il Piraña (Closed Sat midday and Sun; Via Valentini/Via T. Bertini; Tel. 057 42 57 46; Category 1)* primarily serves seafood. The *biscotti*, Prato's famous almond biscuits, can be purchased at *Biscottificio Mattei* in *Via Ricasoli, 20–22*. *Information: Via Cairoli, 48/52, 59100 Prato; Tel. 057 42 41 12; Fax 05 74 60 79 25*

San Miniato (116/C5)

In mid November this town on the far side of the Arno becomes a truffle mecca. The town has been of strategic importance since the Middle Ages, when Otto I built a castle here, which Friedrich II extended into his massive imperial fortress. The *Duomo* (12th century) with its *museum (Open summer 9 am–12 midday and 3 pm–6 pm Tue–Sun; Winter only Sat and Sun)* and the church of *S. Francesco* are other sights to be visited in this pretty little town. You can dine very well and comfortably at the foot of the mountain at *Il Convio (Closed Wed; Via S. Maiano 2; Tel. 05 71 40 81 14; Category 2–3)*.

Vinci (116/C3, 117/D3)

★ Home town to the great Leonardo. The house where he was born is located in the suburb of *Anchiano* and in the *castle* of Count Guidi one finds the *Biblioteca Leonardiana*, containing all the publications concerning this universal genius. The most fascinating attraction is the *museum*, with its machines, devices and the artist's famous sketches. *Museum open daily 9.30–7 pm; in winter 9.30 am–6 pm; house 3.30 pm–6 pm Thu–Tue; in winter 2.30 pm–5 pm*

Day tours through the land of plenty

These routes are marked in green on the map on the inside front cover and in the Road Atlas beginning on page 104

① MONASTERIES AND MEALS ALONG ROMAN ROADS

 The Via Cassia, today the SS 2, takes you in a southerly direction toward Siena through an ancient cultivated landscape of vineyards, cypress-lined avenues, fortified hamlets, medieval castles, quiet, secluded monasteries and baptismal churches. Leave this route in Colle di Val d'Elsa to head toward the Etruscan city of Volterra and on to S. Gimignano, the 'Jerusalem of Tuscany'. On the way there is time to sample a range of culinary delights in several excellent *trattorie* and have various opportunities to purchase wine and olive oil directly from the producers themselves. The tour covers approximately 190 km and requires a full day.

Start your trip by taking the Via Cassia, the old Roman road (today it's the Strada Statale 2), from Porta Romana in Florence. In *Galluzzo*, even before you have reached the motorway, the figure of the *Certosa* complex rises up on the right-hand side of the road, with its characteristic monastic cells. Built in 1341, the Certosa has a rich collection of art treasures from throughout its eventful past and is definitely worth stopping off to inspect.

For reasons of time you then take the Firenze – Siena Superstrada directly south and leave it again after 18 km at the Tavernelle exit. Having passed through the town itself go about 500 m further on the other side of the town and, on the ridge, make a right-hand turn to *Spoiano*, a wonderful Renaissance villa with an excellent view. The Waspi family runs an agritourism business, selling Colli Senesi wine and first-rate cold-pressed olive oil, both produced without any chemicals whatsoever. *(Tel. 05 58 07 73 13; Fri tours of wine-making facilities).*

Take the road (2) further south towards Poggibonsi and get back on the Superstrada to Siena at Poggibonsi Nord. Then take this until the Colle di Val d'Elsa Nord exit. The town of *Colle di Val d'Elsa* has a medieval quarter, Colle Alta, with the church of *S. Caterina* (15th century), the cathedral square with its *Duomo* (17th century), the Pa-

lazzo Pretorio with its heraldic façade (building commenced in the 13th century) and housing the *Archaeological Museum*, the *Castello* (12th century) and the *Palazzo dei Priori*, containing the *Pinacoteca*. At the foot of the hill, Colle Basso has the church of *S. Agostino* (13th century), a truly special gem. The town is generally known as a crystal polishing centre and since the 15th century also as a centre for printing books.

From here follow the signs to Volterra. The road (68) has a number of sharp bends which offer spectacular views over the fascinating, bare and sparsely populated countryside toward the ancient Etruscan city of *Volterra (page 44)*. After sightseeing in the city (approx. 1–2 hours) follow the signs to Balze. On both sides of the road you can see the remnants of *Etruscan walls* and on the left-hand side there is the church of *S. Giusto* (on the edge of a landslide (parking area).

The road offers glimpses of Volterra receding into the distance as you descend into the valley through the Macchia and low forest in the direction of S. Gimignano. Ten km before reaching the town, turn left toward Gambassi Terme at the intersection near Castagno. After only a few metres the *Osteria Il Castagno* appears on the left-hand side of the road *(Closed Mon; Tel. 05 71 67 80 45; Category 3)*. A little further past this restaurant the road turns left to *S. Vivaldo* (5 km), where directly after the placename sign the road to the right takes you toward *Convento*. Here in this high fir forest surround-

ing the monastery there are 21 chapels, each of which has life-size, multicoloured terracotta figures depicting the life and passion of Christ. They stem from the 16th century, as do both the church and the monastery. Two padres watch over this valuable legacy today and Padre Luigi sells the best honey in Tuscany. At the *Trattoria Il Focolare* you receive a warm welcome and a hot meal *(Only open 6.30 pm-12 midnight Mon-Thu, except for large groups; Tel. 057 16 94 98; Category 3)*. Taking the road from S. Vivaldo further for 4.5 km in a north-westerly direction, you reach *Castelfalfi;* with the most beautiful yet most difficult 18-hole *golf course* in all of Tuscany. There is also fishing, a pool and overnight accommodation *(Tel. 05 71 69 80 93)*.

Back on the main road the other side of Castagno, turn left at the intersection toward S. Gimignano. After only a few metres a picture-book cypress-lined avenue takes you to the *Ristorante Casa Al Chino* with a panoramic restaurant and reasonably priced rooms *(Closed Thu; Tel. 05 77 94 60 22; Category 2–3)*. After driving another 50 m along this road, take the dirt road on the left for 2.5 km to the *Fattoria La Torre*, a medium-sized estate selling wine and olive oil, grappa and a whole variety of herbs and sauces. The *Fattoria Ponte a Rondolino Teruzzi e Puthod* at the foot of *S. Gimignano (page 42)* produces 500,000 bottles of the region's best wine. The town's towers come into view soon after you get back onto the tarred road. Reach the *fattoria* on foot from S. Gimignano by following the signs to the left (keep left until you reach the *fattoria* in the valley).

On the way back drive around S. Gimignano to the right until you reach Porta S. Giovanni with a patrolled parking area and, after a tour of the town (1–2 hours), return to Poggibonsi and then to Florence via the Superstrada.

② THROUGH THE LAND OF THE BLACK COCKEREL

 On both sides of the 'Strada del Chianti' (SS222) between Florence and Siena there are innumerable signs to the *fattorie*, the vineyards. Wine can be bought practically everywhere and it's generally of high quality. You'll be taking in two delightful villas and three vineyards which have made names for themselves with particularly good wines – quality products for connoisseurs but at a price. The tour is only 120 km but you should pencil in a whole day in order not to rush any wine tastings.

You leave Florence via the Porta Romana and drive past the Villa Imperiale before heading south through the delightful *campagna fiorentina* between olive groves, villas and tiny hamlets in the direction of *Impruneta (page 41)*. Once in the town turn right after the church toward Ferrone (not toward Greve, so continue straight ahead at the fork near the new buildings). The road takes you through classic Tuscan countryside and drops down before following the Greve River.

The vineyards start here and you'll see the first signs. Just after Passo dei Pecorai you can't miss the one to *Castello di Vicchiomaggio (Tel. 055 85 40 79; Fax*

055 85 39 11). Turn left here before taking a sharp right-hand turn at the foot of the hill onto the dirt road to the Castello. If you can't wait then drop in to the *Cantina S. Jacopo* to supplement your wine collection, but the drive up to the highly-visible castle is worth the extra wait. There are various activities to engage in here: taking tours of the old winery and cellars or buying wine (the two reds Riserva Petri and Ripa delle More both show great potential), grappa and the full-flavoured *olio di oliva extra vergine*, of which about 7,000 litres is produced annually at Vicchiomaggio. Typical Tuscan fare of the finest quality (but at reasonable prices) is served in its elegant dining rooms. You can book rooms to stay for just a single night and even get married in their small chapel.

From the garden you can see the old *Castello di Verrazzano (Tel. 055 85 42 43; Fax 055 85 42 41)* on the opposite hill. To get there just follow the main road back and then turn right onto the entrance road after only a few metres. There is also a stall where you can buy wine right on the road, but as before it is better to go up the gravel road to the Castello.

The Verrazzano vineyards are first mentioned in a manuscript from 1170 but in recent years their *barrique wines* Sassello, Querciolino and Particolare have proved to be a sensation among wine buffs. The castle and charming gardens are accessible to the public and there are wine tastings and tours of the cellars.

Back on the SS222 again you come after only a few kilometres to *Greve (page 41)*, the main town of the Chianti region with a lovely market square. Make sure you visit the *Antica Macelleria Falorni* under the arcades of the Piazza. Having started out generations ago as a simple butcher shop, the *Macelleria* has become an internationally renowned gourmet paradise with a full range of the region's culinary delights. Small, tasty snacks are available at the *Enoteca Gallo Nero* at the northern end of the Piazza *(Closed Thu; Via G. Battisti; Tel. 055 85 37 34, Category 2)*.

The next town along the SS222 is *Panzano (page 42)*. At a point somewhere above the Piazza a narrow road heads toward Mercatale. After the chapel turn left and take the road in the direction of S. Lucia, and then drive about 1 km through vineyards down an untarred road until you come to the *Fattoria di Rampolla (Tel. 055 85 20 01)*. The wines produced by the family of the Principe Di Napoli Rampolla on this 42-hectare vineyard are considered unequivocally to be among the best in Tuscany. According to Italy's leading wine guru, Luigi Veronelli, their Sammarco Cabernet Sauvignon is a 'big, bold wine with rare and distinct character which can be cellared for years'. The Chianti Classico Riserva also falls into the 3-star category. The whole family works in the vineyard, so you may have to wait a few minutes for someone to turn up to give a tour of the cellars or sell you some wine. But the wait is definitely worth it!

Three km after Panzano turn left to Radda in Chianti, in order to reach the next vineyard. Drive along the Pesa River through vineyards and woods until after about 10 km where you take a left at a hairpin bend up a windy road to *Castello di Volpaia (Tel. 05 77 73 80 66)*. In just a few years the owners have turned this previously deserted village into one of the best known vineyards and a mecca of modern art. The wines (red: Nero di Volpaia, Balifico and especially the Coltassala; white: Torniello) and excellent olive oil are sold throughout the year on the tiny village square. In the autumn and winter months, art exhibitions are held in the Commenda.

Via *Radda in Chianti (page 42)* the road takes you through forests and down to *Castellina (page 41)* where on the outskirts there is a sharp right turn to S. Donato. The road then heads across a very high plateau with wonderful views for 7 km until you come to a turn-off to Olena. After taking this road for 1 km turn left again to Monsanto and the *Cantine Isole e Olena*. Paolo De Marchis's best wine is the Cepparello, which is made from 100-per cent Sangiovese grapes, but the typical Tuscan dessert wine, the Vin Santo of Isole e Olena is also famous. Tastings and purchases can be made at any time but groups are requested to make a prior booking *(Tel. 05 58 07 27 63; Fax 05 58 07 22 36)*.

If you are undertaking this tour in summer and you have any time left, do listen to a concert in the Romanesque chapel of *S. Donato* before taking the Superstrada back to your breathtaking point of departure, Florence.

Practical information

*This chapter lists all the essential addresses and information
you need for your Tuscan holiday*

AMERICAN & BRITISH ENGLISH

Marco Polo travel guides are written in British English. In North America, certain terms and usages deviate from British usage. Some of the more frequently encountered examples are:
baggage for *luggage*, *billion* for *milliard*, *cab* for *taxi*, *car rental* for *car hire*, *drugstore* for *chemist's*, *fall* for *autumn*, *first floor* for *groundfloor*, *freeway/highway* for *motorway*, *gas(oline)* for *petrol*, *railroad* for *railway*, *restroom* for *toilet/lavatory*, *streetcar* for *tram*, *subway* for *underground/tube*, *toll-free numbers* for *freephone numbers*, *trailer* for *caravan*, *trunk* for *boot*, *vacation* for *holiday*, *wait staff* for *waiting staff (in restaurants etc.)*, *zip code* for *postal code*.

ACCOMMODATION

Agriturismo
This is the Italian version of a farm holiday and is becoming increasingly popular. There are 1,450 Tuscan villas and renovated farm houses to choose from. A recent innovation is a grading system using heads of wheat (1–5) to indicate the category. Two booking agents which can be recommended are: *Calcione Castle & Country (Via*

Giusti, 34, 50121 Firenze; Tel. and Fax 05 52 34 47 45) and *Salogi Villas, Farmhouses & Apartments (Via S. Gregorio, 5, 55100 Lucca; Tel. 058 34 87 17; Fax 058 34 87 27)*. You can also receive a wide ranging list from *Agriturist (Via dei Barberi, 108, 58100 Grosseto; Tel. and. Fax 05 64 41 74 18)*. Don't book too late!

Camping
You are not allowed to camp outside designated camping areas in Italy. There are, however, 160 registered camping parks and everyone should be able to find something to suit their needs. The 'Carta d'Italia Parchi Campeggio' (map of sites) is available from ENIT offices. Information from *Federcampeggio (Via Vittorio Emanuele, 11, 50041 Calenzano; Tel. 055 88 23 91)*.

Hotels
As of 1999 it is possible to book any hotel room in Italy by dialling the tollfree number *00 49 01 67 01 57 72 (only within Italy) (Mon–Fri 9 am–8 pm)*.

Youth hostels
There are around a dozen youth hostels in Tuscany. Information: *Associazione Italiana Alberghi per la Gioventù (Via Cavour, 44, 00184 Roma; Tel. 0039/06 487 11 52)*

BOATING

If your motorboat has more than a 3-HP motor you will require third-party personal liability insurance. Sailing boats, motorboats and pedal boats *(pedali)* can be hired in the seaside resorts.

BUS

Buses run between most towns in Tuscany. You can catch them on most main railway squares and other large squares in smaller towns.

CAR HIRE/CAR RENTAL

Avis, Hertz and Maggiore all have offices in Florence, Pisa and Livorno, while the first two also have ones in Siena. Hertz also has an office in Piombino, Avis is present in Porto S. Stefano, Prato, Viareggio and Porto Azzurro on Elba, Maggiore in Cecina, Grosseto, Lucca und Portoferraio (Elba). Daily rental prices for a small car begin at around L120,000 and a week's rental costs at least L500,000.

CONSULATES & EMBASSIES

Canadian Embassy
Via G.B. de Rossi, 27, 00161 Roma, Italia, Tel: (39) 6 44 59 81, Fax: (39) 6 44 59 87 54

American Consulate General, Florence
Lungarno A. Vespucci, 38, 50123 Firenze, Tel: (39) 055 23 98 27 6/7/8/9, Fax: (39) 055 28 40 88

American Embassy, Rome
Via Vittorio Veneto 119/A 00187 Roma Tel: (39) 064 67 41

Fax: (39) 064 88 26 72 or 06 46 74 23 56

British Consulate
Consolato Britannico Lungarno Corsini 2 50123 Firenze FI Tel: Centralino: 055 28 41 33 Fax: 055 21 91 12

CURRENCY

The banks in larger towns and cities are usually open Mon–Fri from 8.20 am–1.20 pm and 2.45 pm–3.45 pm. On a town's name-day, and on 14 Aug, 24 and 31 Dec they are only open from 8.20 am–11.20 am. The savings banks *(casse di risparmio)* in smaller towns only tend to open in the morning. Eurocheques can be cashed for amounts up to L300,000 per cheque and the same amount can be withdrawn at cashpoint machines bearing the Eurocheque logo. Major travellers cheques are accepted at banks and there is a minimum commission charge, so changing small amounts is uneconomical. Some establishments are loath to accept cheques in lire as doing so is less profitable for the exchanger than accepting sterling or dollars. Many restaurants, large hotels, shops, petrol (gas) stations, and motorway toll booths accept credit cards.

CUSTOMS

Within the EU travellers may take any goods for their personal use in or out of countries. The guidelines are generally 800 cigarettes, 90 litres of wine (a maximum of 60 litres of sparkling wine) and 10 litres of spirits.

The following goods bought duty-free may be imported into

Italy by passengers from EU countries and other countries without incurring customs duty: 200 cigarettes or 50 cigars or 100 cigarillos or 250 g of tobacco; 750 ml of spirits (over 22%) or 2 litres of fortified or sparkling wine; 60 g of perfume and 250 ml of eau de toilette; 500 g of coffee or 200 g of coffee extract; 100 g of tea or 40 g of tea extract.

DRIVING

The speed limit on highways is 130 km/h, on highways 110 km/h, on country roads 90 km/h, and in municipal areas 50 km/h. The blood alcohol limit is 0.8. Seatbelts must be worn at all times in Italy.

Petrol (gas) prices in Italy are relatively high. Petrol stations are open on workdays from the hours of 7.30 am–12.30 pm and 3 pm–7 pm. On Sunday you will only find them open on some main roads out of the cities and along the highways. You must always carry your driving licence and car registration papers. It is recommended that you have the green insurance card and under some circumstances international travel insurance documents.

You must pay a toll to use any of the highways but not the expressway *(superstrade)*. A one-way trip in a car along the Brennero–Firenze stretch of the highway will incur a toll of at least L40,000 and the Chiasso–Firenze stretch at least L30,000. To this you can add the tolls for using the Austrian or Swiss highways to get there. Austria sells highway stickers for various periods of time and prices and a Swiss sticker for the current year costs around EURO 25.00. To avoid long waits at highway toll booths you can buy pre-paid magnetic swipe cards *(Viacards)* at the

Italian border or from ACI offices and tobacconists for L50,000, L100,000 or L 150,000. The Viacards are valid for an unlimited period. Throughout Italy the official breakdown service *(Tel. 116)* is free of charge.

EMERGENCIES

The following numbers can be dialled free of charge from any telephone:
Carabinieri (for crimes) 112
Fire Brigade (Vigili del fuoco) 115
Ambulance 118
Police (for accidents/with paramedics) 113
Breakdown service 116

FERRIES

Livorno is the largest ferry harbour in Tuscany (pay close attention to the signs as there are two check-in areas). Toremar provides services to the islands of Capraia, Elba, Gorgona and Pianosa (also ferries to Sardinia and Corsica). From Piombino there are direct ferries *(traghetti)* and hydrofoils *(aliscafi)* to Elbe run by Toremar, Elbaferries and Moby Lines. From Porto S. Stefano on the Monte Argentario peninsula there are connections to Giglio and Giannutri using Toremar and Maregiglio. Cars can be taken on ferries to Elba, Capraia and Giglio (usually only if you're staying at least two weeks). You must book early – especially in high season!

Elbaferries
Piombino; Tel. 05 65 22 09 56; Fax 05 65 22 09 96

Maregiglio
Porto S. Stefano; Tel. and Fax 05 64 81 29 20

Moby Lines

Piombino; Tel. 05 65 22 12 12; Fax 05 65 91 67 58

Toremar

Livorno; Tel. 05 86 89 61 13; Fax 05 86 88 72 63
Piombino; Tel. 056 53 11 00; Fax 05 65 59 03 87
Porto S. Stefano; Tel. 05 64 81 46 15; Fax 05 64 59 01 97

HEALTH

Pharmacies

Pharmacies *(farmacia)* have a list of names and addresses on their doors indicating which pharmacies are open outside normal trading hours.

Health insurance

If you are a citizen of the EU you should take your EU E111 form with you, which is available from your health insurance provider. In any other situation you should make sure you have health coverage in your travel insurance.

INFORMATION

Italian State Tourist Office (ENIT)
In Great Britain:

Italian State Tourist Office (ENIT)
1 Princes Street, London W1R 8AY
Tel: (0171) 408 12 54
(recorded message, press 1 to bypass)
or (0891) 60 02 80 (brochure line, calls are charged at 50p per minute).
Fax: (0171) 493 66 95.
Web site: http://www.enit.it
Opening hours: 9 am–5 pm Mon–Fri

In the United States:

Italian State Tourist Office (ENIT)
Suite 1565, 630 Fifth Avenue, New York, NY 10111
Tel: (212) 245 56 18.
Fax: (212) 586 92 49.
Web site: http://www.enit.it

In Canada:

Italian State Tourist Office (ENIT)
Suite 1914, 1 Place de Ville Marie, Montréal, Québec H3B 2C3
Tel: (514) 866 76 67
Fax: (514) 392 14 29

In Tuscany at the Azienda di Promozione Turistica (APT) in each provincial capital.

MEASURES & WEIGHTS

1 cm	0.39 inch
1 m	1.09 yd (3.28 ft)
1 km	0.62 miles
1 m²	1.20 yd²
1 ha	2.47 acres
1 km²	0.39 mi²
1 g	0.035 ounces
1 kg	2.21 pounds
1 British tonne	*1016 kg*
1 US ton	*907 kg*

1 litre is equivalent to 0.22 Imperial gallons and 0.26 US gallons

NEWSPAPERS

You can get current English-language newspapers and magazines at many stands and newsagents in Florence. In Livorno this is not always the case, and in smaller towns you may only get them during the tourist season at large stands – and then they may be a few days old.

OPENING HOURS

In Italy shops are not required to close at a particular time. Most shops open at 8.30 am or 9 am and close again around 7.30 pm. Apart from the large supermarkets they tend to be closed for lunch from 12.30/1 pm–3.30/4 pm. In tourist towns and cities many businesses are open late into the night. Churches tend to be open from 8 am–12 midday and 3–6 pm.

PASSPORT & VISA

Tourists from Great Britain, Canada and the USA only require a valid passport.

PETS

Dogs and cats require certificates of health (not older than 30 days) and a rabies inoculation certificate (at least 30 days but no more than 11 months old). Dogs are not allowed in most restaurants, shops and many beaches.

POST OFFICE & TELEPHONE

Post offices are generally open Mon–Fri from 8.15 am–1.40 pm and Saturday until 12.20 pm. Stamps (*francobolli*) can also be bought from tobacconists and in bars displaying the large T sign.

In the country you can make phone calls in bars displaying a large, white telephone dial. Payment is normally by means of a telephone card, but sometimes with coins, and even with the special L200 telephone chips (*gettoni*). Almost all telephone booths take only magnetic phone cards, which you can buy at bars, tobacconists and post offices for L5,000, L10,000 and L15,000. Note: Before using them you have to tear off the perforated corner!

To phone abroad you first need to dial 00 and then the international dialling code for the country required: Canada and United States 1; Ireland: 353; United Kingdom 44. To call Italy from abroad you need to first dial 0039 (01139 from the USA). As there are no longer any dialling codes within Italy you always have to dial a zero before the number you are trying to reach, even if calling from another country.

SPORTS

Fishing
You can fish in the sea without a permit but one is required for inland waterways or lakes (inquire at any APT office).

Mountain climbing
The Club Alpino Italiano (CAI) conducts climbing tours in the Apuan Alps, as well as mountain and general hiking tours. *CAI, Via dello Studio, 5, 50122 Firenze; Tel. 05 52 39 85 80*

Golf
There are golf courses in Ugolino south of Florence, in Punta Ala, Montecatini Terme, Acquabona on Elba, in Tirrenia, Pietrasanta, Castelfalfi and Chianciano Terme (to name but a few).

Horse riding
Horse riding is available on many farms offering *agriturismo*, at coastal resorts, and in Florence, Montecatini, Siena and Montepulciano.

Sailing and windsurfing
There are schools in most seaside resort towns and on the islands.

Skiing
Skiing is usually possible until Easter at Monte Amiata, in the Apuan Alps, at Abetone (Pistoia) and at Monte Secchieta, east of Florence.

Diving
Most diving schools are on Elba and Giglio. Expert divers do not require a licence and there are excellent spots in marked areas on the islands and along the Etruscan Riviera.

Tennis

Every city and spa or seaside resort has tennis courts. Large hotels have their own private ones.

Hiking

The mountains in the Garfagnana near Lucca, the area around Monte Amiata, the Chianti hills and the coastal nature reserves are all excellent places for hiking. If you're doing any hiking or stopping in at farms don't forget there are vipers throughout Tuscany. Please follow these simple rules, especially from May–October: wear closed footwear (especially children) and never stick your hands into a pile of leaves, wood or rocks without banging it with a stick beforehand. If, however, you do happen to get bitten by a viper: apply a tourniquet, suck the poison out, remain calm – and head to the closest hospital (ospedale) as soon as possible.

TIPPING

Many restaurants include a cover charge in the bill, so it is up to your own discretion whether you tip on top of this or not. Where there is no cover charge, for example in bars, 12–15 % is usual. One generally pays the bill and then leaves the tip from the change on the tray or table.

VOLTAGE

220V AC, with two-pin, round-pronged plugs.

WEATHER IN FLORENCE

Seasonal averages

Daytime temperatures in °C/F

Jan	Feb	Mar	Apr	May	June	July	Aug	Sept	Oct	Nov	Dec
8/46	10/50	14/57	19/66	23/73	28/82	31/88	30/86	26/79	19/66	13/55	9/48

Night-time temperatures in °C/F

Jan	Feb	Mar	Apr	May	June	July	Aug	Sept	Oct	Nov	Dec
2/36	3/37	6/43	9/48	13/55	16/61	19/66	19/66	16/61	12/54	7/45	3/37

Sunshine: hours per day

Jan	Feb	Mar	Apr	May	June	July	Aug	Sept	Oct	Nov	Dec
4	4	5	6	7	9	10	9	7	6	4	4

Rainfall: days per month

Jan	Feb	Mar	Apr	May	June	July	Aug	Sept	Oct	Nov	Dec
9	7	8	8	9	6	3	4	6	9	11	9

Do's and don'ts!

*Even in Tuscany there are things
you should and should not do*

Pickpockets

Opportunity makes the thief: Never leave cameras, binoculars or any new purchases in your car where they can be seen. And don't put too much trust in the security of your car trunk either, especially at night if yours is a rental vehicle. Car radios should also be removed before parking if possible.

Begging

Beggars can become a nuisance, especially in the cities. Make sure your money and important documents are well stashed away, so you don't waste your time repeatedly checking the whereabouts of these valuables. If you wish to give to beggars, just keep a few coins in your pocket – never pull your whole wallet or purse out.

Sunday driving

Know where you're going and try not to drive too slowly while sightseeing – you'll only upset the busy local drivers. It's better to stop to enjoy the view or check a map.

Reckless swimming

While at the beach always pay attention to the lifeguards. If the red flag is flying (e.g. rough seas)

even good swimmers should not venture out further than 10 m from shore, as every beach has its own dangers which only locals are aware of (and which are often invisible to the naked eye). Also check apparently safe beaches before letting small children into the water, as many beaches have undercurrents and channels close to the shore. And when swimming in inland rivers, it is best to be cautious. If it suddenly starts to rain, a small stream can turn into a raging torrent in seconds.

Markets and designer names

You can certainly get some real bargains at markets when it comes to clothes and accessories. But don't be fooled by designer labels at amazing prices! Lacoste shirts are never really from Lacoste – despite the attached crocodile. The same goes for Gucci, Pucci and all the others. It might look good now, but wait till you see it after the first wash at home.

Churches and monasteries

Do not enter them in unacceptable clothing (short pants, bare shoulders) and do not speak or eat during mass.

Road Atlas of Tuscany

*Please refer to back cover for an overview
of this Road Atlas*

D | **E** | **F**

16

Mad d. Bosco
Casal Borsetti
S. Alberto
Marina Romea
Alfonsine
Belricetto
Stella Romea
Porto Corsini
Marina di Ravenna ★

Fusignano
t' Agáta anterno
Villanova
309

LUGO **Bagnacavallo**
309d
Punta Marina
Lido Adriano
67

Lugo Cotignola
Godo Ravenna
RAVENNA ★★

Cotignola
33
S. Apollinare in Classe
A D R I A T I C O

Faenza
Russi
67
Parco Regionale
del Delta del Po

NZA
129
27
Ghibullo
16
Lido di Classe ★
Lido del Savio

Coccolía
Villa-fránca di Forlì
S. Pietro in Vínc.
Sávio

34
Castiglione d. Rav.
CÉRVIA ★

Forlì
Casemurate
254
10
51

9
Carpinello
Cesena-Nord
Cesenático ★

FORLÌ
Forlimpópoli
74
71 b

Castrocaro
67
19
Cesena
304
Gatteo a Mare ★
Bellária

gliana
310
CESENA
18
Igea Marina

Dovádola
Bertinoro
71
E55
14

Méldola
30
7

Predáppio
Savignano sul Rubicone
Viserba

Casciano
E45
RIMINI

C. di Centoforche
310
Santarcángelo di Rom.
A14

re
24
Rimini Sud
72

Civitella di Rom
Sogliano
al Rubicone
Strada
23

Galeata
Rivoschio Pieve
Verucchio

Sofia
Nazionale delle Foreste
SAN MARINO

Spinello
969
Sársina
Mercato Saraceno
San Marino

ési-Monte Faltefona
ampigna
22
55
★★

776
Sant'Ágata Feltria
San Leo
Novaféltria
Mercati

829
M o n t e f e l t r o

S. Piero in Bagno
Álfero
Monte Cerignone
Auditore

sso dei ndrioli
Bagno di Romagna
(490)
Pennabilli
986
Macerata Feltria
15

1173
Vergheréto
Casteldelci
Monte
1415
Carpegna
Foglia

Válico Montecoronaro ratáglia di Serra
1291
853
Carpegna
Sassocorvaro
5

la Verna ★
Balze
258
Frontino
Lunano

208
E45
M d Zucca
1263
988
Badia Tedalda
Sestino
Piandimeleto

Chiusi di Verna
3bis
E45
Passo di Viamággio
S. Ángelo in Vado
17

Pieve S. Stéfano
Borgo Pace
E78
73bis
Urbánia

Caprese Michelángelo
Lámoli
Mercatello sul Metáuro
★

71
Lago di Montedoglio
Boca Trabária
1049
Pióbbico
6

Subbiano
Anghiari
107
A. 111
19

MARE

10 km
5 mi

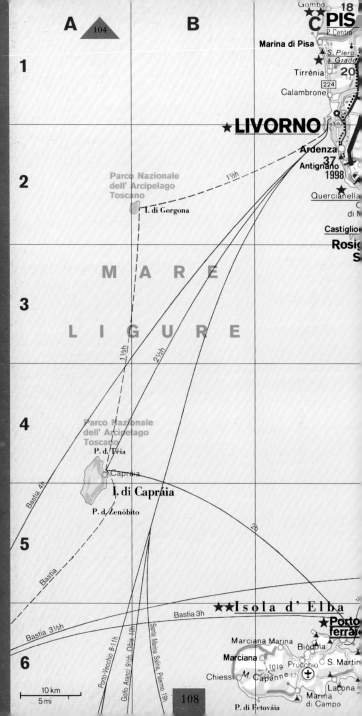

A 104 B C PIS

Gombo 18
P. Centro

Marina di Pisa
S. Piero
a. Grado

1 Tirrénia 20
224
Calambrone

★ **LIVORNO**

Ardenza 37
Antignano
1998

2 Parco Nazionale
dell' Arcipelago
Toscano
1½h
I. di Gorgona

Quercianella

Castiglio

Rosig
S

M A R E

3 **L I G U R E**

1½h 2½h

4 Parco Nazionale
dell' Arcipelago
Toscano
P. d. Teia
Capraia
I. di Capráia
P. d. Zenóbito

2h

5

Bastia 4h

Bastia

Bastia 3½h Bastia 3h ★★ I s o l a d' E l b a

★ **Porto
ferrái**

Marciana Marina Biódola

Marciana Prucchio S. Martin
1019
Chiessi M. Capanne 17

Lacona
Marina
di Campo
P. di Fetováia

6

Porto-Vecchio 8-11h Golfo Aranci 9½h Olbia 10h Santa Marina Salina Palermo 19h

10 km
5 mi

108

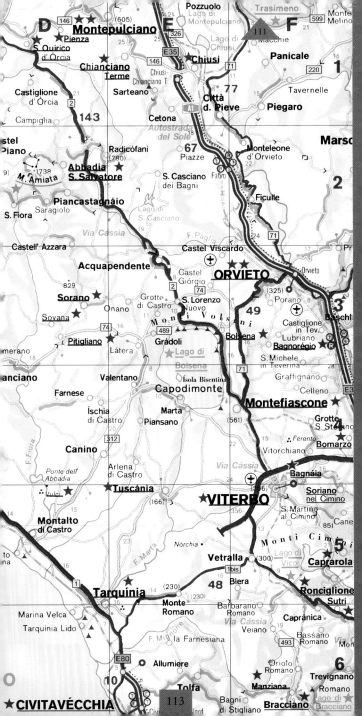

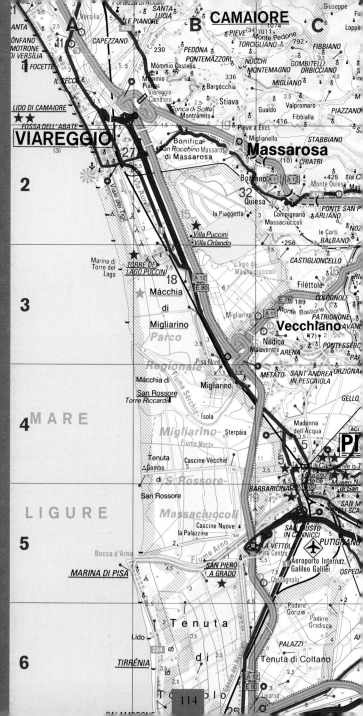

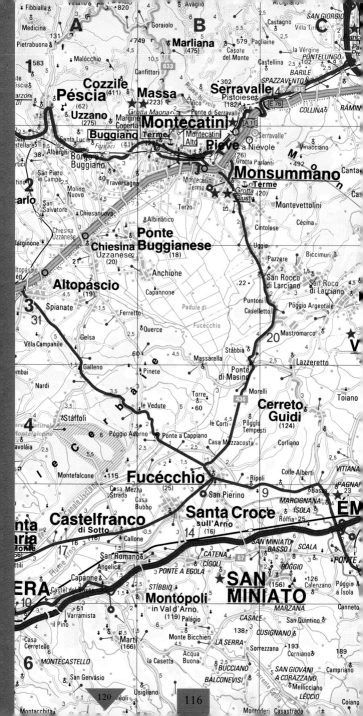

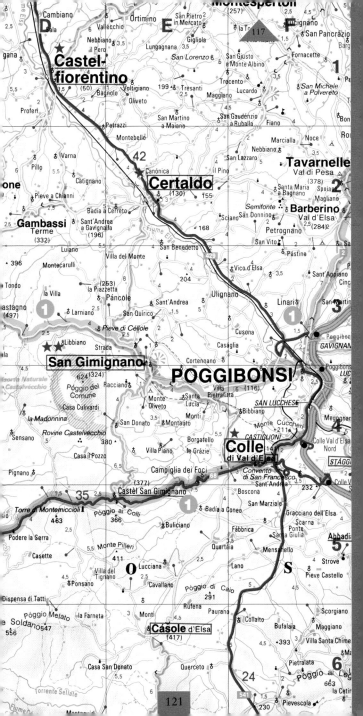

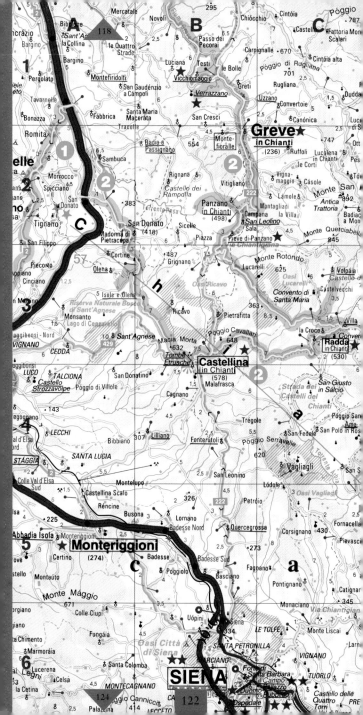

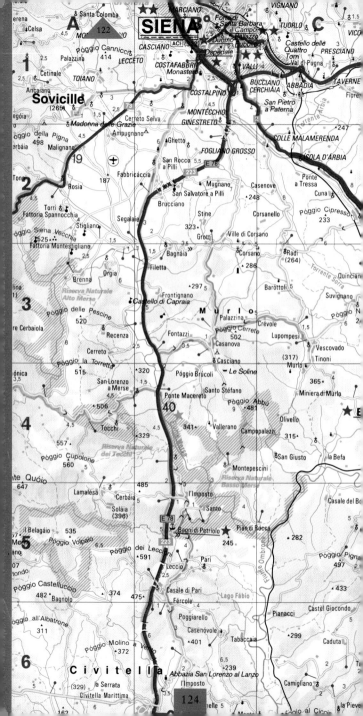

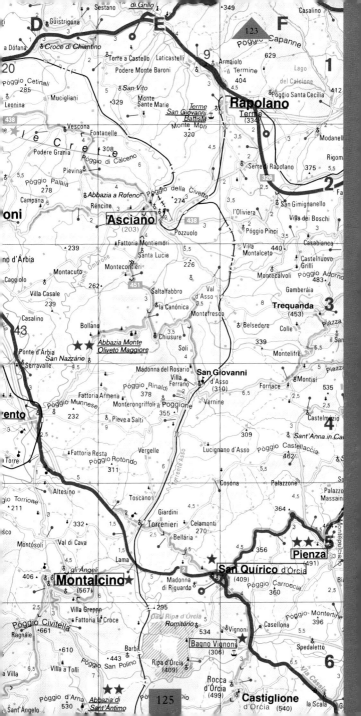

ROAD ATLAS LEGEND

Autobahn · Gebührenpflichtige Anschlußstelle · Gebührenstelle · Anschlußstelle mit Nummer · Rasthaus mit Übernachtung · Raststätte · Erfrischungsstelle · Tankstelle · Parkplatz mit und ohne WC	Trento · ® ® ® ℗ ℗ ℗	Motorway · Toll junction · Toll station · Junction with number · Motel · Restaurant · Snackbar · Filling-station · Parking place with and without WC
Autobahn in Bau und geplant mit Datum der Verkehrsübergabe	Datum Date	Motorway under construction and projected with completion date
Zweibahnige Straße (4-spurig)		Dual carriageway (4 lanes)
Bundesstraße · Straßennummern	E45	Federal road · Road numbers
Wichtige Hauptstraße		Important main road
Hauptstraße · Tunnel · Brücke	⊃=⊂	Main road · Tunnel · Bridge
Nebenstraßen		Minor roads
Fahrweg · Fußweg		Track · Footpath
Wanderweg (Auswahl)		Tourist footpath (selection)
Eisenbahn mit Fernverkehr		Main line railway
Zahnradbahn, Standseilbahn		Rack-railway, funicular
Kabinenschwebebahn · Sessellift		Aerial cableway · Chair-lift
Autofähre	●	Car ferry
Personenfähre		Passenger ferry
Schiffahrtslinie		Shipping route

German	Symbol	English
Naturschutzgebiet · Sperrgebiet		Nature reserve · Prohibited area
Nationalpark, Naturpark · Wald		National park, natural park · Forest
Straße für Kfz gesperrt	X X X X X X	Road closed to motor vehicles
Straße mit Gebühr		Toll road
Straße mit Wintersperre	XII-II	Road closed in winter
Straße für Wohnanhänger gesperrt bzw. nicht empfehlenswert	🚫 ⟨🚫 🚫⟩ ⟨🚫	Road closed or not recommended for caravans
Touristenstraße · Paß	Weinstraße ⌃1510	Tourist route · Pass
Schöner Ausblick · Rundblick · Landschaftlich bes. schöne Strecke	☆ ☀	Scenic view · Panoramic view · Route with beautiful scenery

German	Symbol	English
Golfplatz · Schwimmbad	⛳ —	Golf-course · Swimming pool
Ferienzeltplatz · Zeltplatz	▲ ▲	Holiday camp · Transit camp
Jugendherberge · Sprungschanze	△ ⚲	Youth hostel · Ski jump
Kirche im Ort, freistehend · Kapelle	⚭ ⚬	Church · Chapel
Kloster · Klosterruine	⚑ ⚑	Monastery · Monastery ruin
Schloß, Burg · Schloß-, Burgruine	⚑ ⚑	Palace, castle · Ruin
Turm · Funk-, Fernsehturm	⌶ �📡	Tower · Radio-, TV-tower
Leuchtturm · Kraftwerk	⌶ ⚡	Lighthouse · Power station
Wasserfall · Schleuse	⟼ ┼	Waterfall · Lock
Bauwerk · Marktplatz, Areal	▫	Important building · Market place, area
Ausgrabungs- u. Ruinenstätte · Feldkreuz	∴ ✝	Arch. excavation, ruins · Calvary
Dolmen · Menhir	π ◊	Dolmen · Menhir
Hünen-, Hügelgrab · Soldatenfriedhof	☆ ⊞	Cairn · Military cemetery
Hotel, Gasthaus, Berghütte · Höhle	⌂ ∩	Hotel, inn, refuge · Cave

Kultur / Culture

Kultur	Symbol	Culture
Malerisches Ortsbild · Ortshöhe	**WIEN** (171)	Picturesque town · Height of settlement
Eine Reise wert	★★ **MILANO**	Worth a journey
Lohnt einen Umweg	★ **TEMPLIN**	Worth a detour
Sehenswert	**Andermatt**	Worth seeing

Landschaft / Landscape

Landschaft	Symbol	Landscape
Eine Reise wert	★★ **Las Cañadas**	Worth a journey
Lohnt einen Umweg	★ **Texel**	Worth a detour
	Dikti	Worth seeing

Maßstab für Reiseatlas Seiten 114-125	5 km 2 mi	Scale for Road Atlas pages 114-125

INDEX

This index lists all the main places and sights mentioned in this guide.
Numbers in bold indicate a main entry, italics a photograph

What do you get for your money?

 The unit of currency is the Italian Lira (Lit). The bank notes are in denominations of L500,000, L100,000, L50,000, L10,000, L5,000, L2,000 and L1,000. There are L1,000, L500, L200, L100 and L50 coins. It is easiest to change money in Italy.

For the visitor it is important to know what to expect to pay for admission charges, food and beverages. Here are a few prices to give you an idea of what your money is worth:

A single bus ticket costs L1,500 in Florence, the minimum taxi fare is L6,500, and parking costs about L3,000 for the initial hour. Museum tickets vary between L2,000 and L15,000, but those under 18 or over 60 or 65 usually get in free of charge. In Pisa you also have to pay L2,000 to enter the Duomo. A movie ticket costs at least L13,000, a seat at the opera anywhere from L30,000 and up to L100,000 for festival tickets. A little cheaper are the troupes of performers plying their trade in rural areas during the summer months and charging as little as L5,000. Discos tend to be expensive, especially in seaside resort towns, costing you around L20,000 just to get in. One hour of horse riding also costs about L20,000. An ice-cream (gelato) costs upward of L3,000, a cup of espresso at least L1,200, and a cappuccino between L1,500 and L10,000, depending on where you're sitting (or standing).

US$	Italian Lira (L)	£	Italian Lira (L)	Can$	Italian Lira (L)
1	1,795	1	2,904	1	1,203
2	3,490	2	5,808	2	2,406
3	5,385	3	8,712	3	3,610
4	7,180	4	11,617	4	4,813
5	8,975	5	14,521	5	6,016
10	17,951	10	29,042	10	12,033
15	26,927	15	43,563	15	18,050
20	35,903	20	58,085	20	24,067
25	44,879	25	72,606	25	30,084
30	53,855	30	87,127	30	36,100
40	71,806	40	116,170	40	48,134
50	89,758	50	145,213	50	60,167
60	107,710	60	174,256	60	72,201
70	125,662	70	203,298	70	84,235
80	143,614	80	232,341	80	96,268
90	161,565	90	261,383	90	108,302
100	179,517	100	290,426	100	120,336
200	359,034	200	580,852	200	240,672
300	538,551	300	871,278	300	361,007
400	718,068	400	1,161,704	400	481,343
500	897,585	500	1,452,130	500	601,679
750	1,346,377	750	2,178,195	750	902,519
1,000	1,795,170	1,000	2,904,260	1,000	1,203,358